CHAMPIONS
OF YOUR CENTURY
1900-1999
by Alan Forrest

As chosen by readers of the
Leicester Mercury

KAIROS PRESS
1999
in association with
Leicester Mercury

First Published in Great Britain by
KAIROS PRESS
552 Bradgate Road, Newtown Linford, Leicestershire LE6 0HB
1999

in association with the Leicester Mercury

Copyright © Leicester Mercury and Alan Forrest, 1999

All rights reserved. No part of this publication may be reproduced, stored in a retrieval system, or transmitted in any form, or by any means, electronic, mechanical, photocopying, recording or otherwise without prior permission in writing of the copyright holders, nor be otherwise circulated in any form or binding or cover other than the one in which it is published and without a similar condition being imposed on the subsequent publisher.

Cover pictures:
Top row: Elvis Presley – photo courtesy BMG Ent.; Celine Dion – photo courtesy of David Pomona, Pomona Music; Laurel and Hardy; Morecambe and Wise – photo courtesy BBC; John Cleese as Basil Fawlty – photo courtesy BBC.
Second Row: Shawdaddywaddy; Dalmation; Joanna Lumley as Patsy in Absolutely Fabulous – photo courtesy BBC; Great Dane puppies – photo from Leicester Mercury.
Third Row: Orson Welles in Citizen Kane, RKO Radio Pictures; Paul Merton in The Lift – photo courtesy Carlton International Media Ltd; Whitney Houston – photo courtesy BMG Arista; Queen Elizabeth II – photo from Leicester Mercury; Michael Jackson – photo courtesy EMI.
Fourth Row: Marilyn Monroe in River Of No Return – photo courtesy BBC; Tommy Cooper; Winston Churchill, photo from Northcliffe Newspapers; Judy Garland and Fred Astaire.

ISBN 1-871344-24-7

First edition 1999

Book design and layout by Robin Stevenson, Kairos Press
Body text in Humanist 521 BT, 11pt
Imagesetting by Dotperfect Reprographics, Leicester
Cover design and film by Geoff Sanders, Creative Design Studio, Leicester Mercury
Printed in Great Britain by Norwood Press, Anstey, Leicester.

Contents

Foreword 4
A Letter from the Author 5
Introduction 6

Part One: The Contenders

Male Comedians 7
Female Comedians 12
Comedy Teams 16
    Best Comedians: What You Said - 21
Breeds of Dog 22
    Dogs: What You Said - 26
War Songs 27
    War Songs: What You Said - 29
Rock Groups 32
    Rock Groups: What You Said - 35
Musicals and Disney Animated Films 36
Cinema Films 40
    Films and Musicals: What You Said - 45
Voices 49
    Voices: What You Said - 51
Pop Singers 52
    Pop Singers: What You Said - 57
Poets 58
Novelists 60
    Poets and Novelists: What You Said - 64
Cinema Stars 65
    Film Stars: What You Said - 71

Part Two: The Champions

Greatest Cinema Stars, Male and Female 72
Greatest Breed of Dog and Greatet Novelist ... 76
Greatest Comedy Team and Greatest War Song . 79
Greatest Rock Group and Speaking Voice 82
Greatest Male and Female Comedians 85
Greatest Musical and Disney Animated Films ... 87
Greatest Cinema Film and Greatest Poet 91
Greatest Pop Singers, Male and Female 94

Index 98

Foreword

People have always loved those conversations (arguments?) that revolve around trying to identify who was the best actor, singer, politician - or whatever - of the century.

As the millennium approached it was impossible for us to resist the temptation to invite every Leicester Mercury reader to join in the debate – and that was the start of our popular Your Century columns.

Nick Carter, Editor-in-chief of the Leicester Mercury

In fact they were so popular that we decided to bring together these highlights, featuring the best of the pages. Whatever your opinion on comedians, film stars, pop singers, novelists, rock bands or breeds of dogs - you will find something to please (or displease) you in this volume.

Whether you sit and read it by yourself or start one of those arguments with family and friends, we hope you enjoy the book.

And rest assured that the Leicester Mercury will continue to keep you at the heart of everything as we enter the new millennium.

A Letter from the Author

Alan Forrest

The Century is best summed up by its cinema stars and the things they said. In 1939 in Gone With The Wind, Scarlett O'Hara asked Rhett Butler: "But if you go, what will I do, what will become of me?"
Clark Gable replied, "Frankly, my dear…." And it became the top cinema Catch Phrase of our Century - until Sean Connery arrived as James Bond and a new Catch Phrase champion was declared. For many years I longed to see them together in one film. Sean Connery would burst in and declare: "My name's Bond, James Bond." And Clark Gable would reply: "Frankly, my dear, I don't give a damn!"

It's amazing how a Catch Phrase can make your fortune. For example, in Four Weddings and a Funeral Hugh Grant became an instant star simply by saying, "excellent….excellent", along, of course, with whatever he muttered each time he overslept on the morning of a wedding.

The real Catch Phrase of the Century would have been "Play it again, Sam," except that nobody actually said it in Casablanca. Ingrid Bergman said: "Play it, Sam, play As Time Goes By." It's a beautiful film and I wouldn't change a word of it but all this could have been avoided if he had simply replied: "I'm sorry but if I play it for you now, pretty soon you'll say 'play it **again**, Sam' and then everyone will be saying it."

The great Catch Phrase from David Lean's masterpiece, Lawrence of Arabia, comes when Peter O'Toole and Bedouin leader Omar Sharif are riding across the desert to capture Akaba. After many hours on a camel in scorching heat, O'Toole begins to fall asleep and is in danger of falling out of the saddle. Omar Sharif wakes him with a flick of his whip and warns: "You were drifting, English."
Very handy if you take your husband to the opera and he nods off and starts to fall forward over the lady in front of him. Hit him on the shoulder and give him the stern warning, "you were drifting, English!"

A proposed Catch Phrase that misfired was in Working Girl in which Melanie Griffith is fed up with her pushy boyfriend and yells: "I am not steak. You cannot order me!" I've never heard anyone say that. By contrast, in the film her boyfriend replies: "I've got priorities, too. When you get yourself together, maybe we can talk. Right now we're history!" Almost by accident this has become a major Catch Phrase of our time.
A woman told me her young daughter was phoned for what would be her first date. The girl was very excited until the lad told her the cinema film he had chosen. After a brief argument she hung up on him. She told her mother: "Perhaps he'll call back and see it my way but right now we're history!"

Clearly the films have had a major impact on our lives over the past 100 years. In any event, may the force be with you in the new Century.

Alan

Introduction

If you always read the last page of a novel first, to see how it comes out, well then by all means check out the final eight chapters for the election results.

However, why spoil the fun? We hope you will start at the beginning and follow along, step by step, to see what your friends and neighbours had to say about the various candidates as we progressed from lists of possible contenders to the selection of the top ten finalists in each category.

WHAT IT'S ALL ABOUT

The search for the sixteen Champions of Your Century featured in this book took four stages to achieve.

First, we listed some obvious candidates and asked your opinion of them.

Second, we asked you to suggest other contenders for the title.

Third, based upon your letters and Internet messages, we were able to determine the finalists. Many of these letters are included in the book.

All three of these stages are outlined in the first thirteen chapters.

Then we held an election by telephone and ballot.
When all the votes were counted, we announced the results, which are printed in full in the final eight chapters. There are two champions revealed in each of these chapters for a total of 16 which explains the format of the end of the book.

Some day you will be at a party and someone will cleverly name all the seven dwarfs from Snow White. However, once you've finished reading this book you will be able to top that performance and amaze your friends by naming all 16 Champions of Your Century. This may lead to fame and fortune or at least a well-deserved round of applause.

ACKNOWLEDGEMENTS

The author would like to thank Robin Stevenson for the imaginative design of all the pages, Geoff Sanders for the attractive cover, Steve England for his invaluable advice and assistance, particularly in the search through many files for photographs, Eileen Bray for her excellent secretarial skills, and Leicester Mercury Editor Nick Carter for believing in the Your Century column and this book.

Other notes of appreciation go to Brian Court, EMI Music Publishing and the Gracie Fields Rochdale Museum for assisting in the search for and location of a Gracie Fields song, to Aeron Thomas for helping with the Dylan Thomas photograph, and to the British Phonographic Industry Ltd for their invaluable assistance.

Almost all the photographs used in this book are either publicity pictures issued to promote films and television programmes or the Leicester Mercury's own news photographs. Full credit to the copyright owner has been included with each picture wherever copyright could be determined. We gratefully offer full acknowledgement to them all, with apologies for any errors or omissions.

I am pleased to dedicate this book to MAUREEN MILGRAM
who first suggested the idea and then helped to
make it happen at every step along the way.

Alan Forrest

PART ONE: THE CONTENDERS

Chapter One

Champions of Your Century : 1900 – 1999

MALE COMEDIANS

When we called an election in Leicestershire and Rutland to name the greatest comedian of the Century, we knew from the beginning it was going to be close.

But it was also going to be a great boost for national morale. Almost all of the world's top comedians are British.

Our search for the major comedians of the Century begins in America in the 1920s where Charlie Chaplin, born and raised in England, was the most famous comedy star of his time, thanks to his great success in cinema films. He was best-known for his wild chases and, in the Gold Rush, for his charming little tabletop dance with two forks and rolls, for legs and feet.

The other towering comedian of the early years in America was Bob Hope. He was born in England but his family emigrated when he was a young lad.

As he tells the story: "I left England as soon as I realised I could never become King."

In his own way, he always remained profoundly British. He enjoyed surprising Americans every now and then with a crisp upperclass "thank you" which he pronounced "then kyou", and was a hit in the film Fancy Pants in which he played an English butler hired to add a bit of tone to a wild west cattle ranch.

Another British comedy genius was Stan Laurel who teamed up with the American Oliver Hardy as Laurel and Hardy.

All these Brits Abroad rose to fame because of the power of the American films.

Here in Britain there were many other early comedians as good or better who were legends in their own land but not widely known around the world.

The chief of these is Max Miller, undoubtedly the king of stand-up comedy.

He often performed in Leicester and many people here remember him fondly.

He impressed almost everyone, including Eric Morecambe who said: "He's the greatest, he's my favourite."

Victoria Wood said, "There will never be another one like him."

Another fan was Frankie Howerd who in 1991 was using a

From Top: Bob Hope in 1977; Peter Sellers (photo courtesy Channel 4); **and Rowan Atkinson as 'The Black Adder'** (photo courtesy BBC).

Max Miller.

variation of a routine that Max Miller had made famous in 1939.

Miller was loud, fast and clever and created the impression he was talking directly to you. He was also a great tease and often came close to being rude but always pulled back at the last minute.

A typical jest: "Mary had two little bears to whom she was most kind. I often saw her bear in front but not her – here now!"

(Similarly, in the 1980s in his famous monologues, Ronnie Corbett would lead his audience on and then stop short and say: "You're making up your own jokes!").

Miller also told about the time he was in Blackpool, looking for a room. The landlady said her hotel was full. "I said, surely you could squeeze me in a back room someplace", and she replied, "I could, but I haven't time right now!"

It is also generally agreed that Britain's Sid Field was one of the top comic actors of the first half century. When the American comedian, Danny Kaye, appeared at the Palladium, he stopped his show to pay tribute to Field as the greatest comic actor of his time.

Among speciality acts of the music hall years the one that created the biggest sensation in Europe (and made some impact in America) was Richard Hearne as Mr. Pastry single-handedly dancing the Quadrille.

Other great British comedians of the early years included Little Tich who, in 1900, was both dazzling and heart-warming in a routine in which he was able to dance in shoes almost three feet long.

Similarly, about 1945, Max Wall was entertaining in a series of funny walks, which were perfected later by John Cleese.

In the 1930s, Robb Wilton was a sensation in various skits. The modern comedian Paul Merton selected Wilton's Fire Hall Sketch as one of his favourites. A woman has come to the Fire Station to report that her house is ablaze. Robb asks her: "What time did the fire start?"

She replies: "I don't know, about 7:30."

Robb replies: "Ah, now; ah, now, see the time now, it's 7:25. If we put down 7:30 on that form, we would be liable to arrive at the fire before it broke out and that's the very thing we try to avoid!"

Three other names must be mentioned from the early years.

One is Tommy Handley, star of the radio show It's That Man Again, with 20 million listeners. The second is George Formby with his comic songs about when he's cleaning windows and also Leaning On a Lamp Post in case a certain little lady walks by.

The third is Tommy Trinder, who will always be remembered for one of the greatest true anecdotes of the Century.

He was in Edinburgh and had the opportunity to entertain the Duke of York who later became King George the Sixth as a result of The Abdication.

Eight years later, when Tommy was top of the bill at The Palladium, the King invited him to Buckingham Palace for a Command Performance.

From Top: Ronnie Barker as Fletcher in 'Porridge' (photo courtesy BBC); **Paul Merton in 'The Lift'** (photo courtesy Carlton International Media Ltd, 1996); **Max Wall in 1988; Jack Dee** (photo courtesy Channel 4); **and Rory Bremner – 'The Greatest Rory Ever Told'** (photo courtesy Channel 4).

Clockwise from top left: Les Dawson (photo courtesy BBC, 1993 – 'In The Psychiatrist's Chair'); **Frankie Howerd in All Change** (photo courtesy Yorkshire Television); **Benny Hill** (Thames Television, photo courtesy Pearson Library).

In the reception line, Tommy reminded the King that the last time he had performed for him was in those modest days as Duke and travelling player in Edinburgh.

The King said: "You've climbed very high since those days!"

Tommy replied: "Well, you haven't done so bad yourself!"

The search for the best comedians of the second half of the Century begins with Benny Hill. He is the only British comedian to become internationally famous without conquering America.

Because he specialised in sight gags, he had millions of fans in nations that didn't understand a word of English.

But he was also a master of the spoken joke.

He was at his very best in a comedy sketch when he told an interviewer: "There are people, right here in our community, who advocate the violent overthrow of the government."

"Bolsheviks!"

"No. it's true I tell you!"

He was so delighted by the success of the routine that the following week he said: "I was out walking at midnight and I saw some men dancing around a tree. They were witches; male witches they was."

"Warlocks!"

"No, it's true I tell you!"

Around the world he continues to be the most widely-known, and controversial, of British comedians.

Peter Sellers is a close second, having risen to fame in films as the bumbling detective, Inspector Clouseau. He was always trying dismal disguises and each one was a recipe for disaster. He bought an outfit to make himself look like the Hunchback of Notre Dame and when he turned on the helium to fill out the costume, of course he couldn't turn it off. Up he went and out the window.

Then there was Tony Hancock. At his best he was very amusing. Doug V. Pither of Leicester Forest East commented: "He was so brilliant on radio and television. I loved The Blood Donor sketch."

Hancock had a number of great programmes teamed with Sid James, who later became a star of the Carry On series. Unfortunately nobody could convince Tony Hancock he was a success and he fretted about it. At last he decided to go to America in search of international fame. Alas, his attempt ended in failure. It was a sad end for one of our best comedians.

In more recent days, Bob Monkhouse said he was thrilled to fly to America on Concorde. "I didn't realise they have real silverware and porcelain crockery.

"We don't even have that at home. Well, we do NOW, obviously!"

It may not be the joke of the Century but the basic idea is at least

In the past thirty years Ronnie Barker seemed to be everywhere, in Open All Hours, Porridge, and with Ronnie Corbett in the Two Ronnies. He also wrote many comedy routines.

British comedians seem to have perfected the concept of bumbling their way to glory. Peter Sellers is the most famous example. But there were others.

Frankie Howerd made a total mess of his first stage performance but got so many laughs he adopted Blundering Through as his style, with great results.

Similarly, Tommy Cooper would promise to pull something magical out of a hat but the trick never worked. He was a terrible magician (on purpose) but wonderful to watch.

He also perfected the Max Miller technique of completing the joke at the half-way point. For example, Cooper related 65 years old and it's always guaranteed to provoke a smile. The same joke was told in the 1930s by pier comedians and in music halls:

"You're going on holiday? We had a grand time a few years back in Brighton.

"Can't remember the name of the hotel. Sheila, run upstairs and look at our towels!"

In the 1966 film, The Family Way, John Mills is up early to bring a breakfast tray to his son and daughter-in-law the morning after their wedding.

He is soon joined by his wife, Marjorie Rhodes, who is critical of his efforts. "Men! Just look at these mugs – British Rail!"

The list of great British comedians goes on and on.

John Cleese carved out an international reputation as the star of Fawlty Towers, alongside Andrew (Manuel) Sachs. Cleese also was a key member of Monty Python, especially in the Dead Parrot sketch.

Top: Charlie Chaplin creates factory meyhem in *Modern Times* (1936, United Artists). **Below: Rowan Atkinson studies the Mercury as a Comic Relief stunt in 1992** (photo from Leicester Mercury).

Left: Angus Deayton in 'The Temptation Game' in 1998
(Photo courtesy Talkback Television/BBC Manchester)
Centre: Tommy Cooper got a laugh "just like that".
Right: Joe Pasquale.

how he had found an old violin and a painting and took them to an expert. "He told me I had a Stradivarius and a Rembrandt. UNFORTUNATELY…"

And from that point on it was only a matter of time before everyone in the audience understood the joke before Cooper could complete the sentence, which, of course, ended: "He told me Rembrandt made rotten violins and Stradivarius was a terrible painter."

The joke is similar to the famous British routine about the elderly man who goes into a small chemist shop to buy a potty to put under the bed. The clerk says, "I'm sorry, we don't have any potties. Have you tried Boots?" (Any reply will do).

The long list of great British comedians also includes the all dancing, all singing, all joking Bruce Forsyth, Michael Barrymore, Brian Conley and Des O'Connor.

Ken Dodd is another British comedian of many talents and he's always willing to give helpful advice to young men just starting out. "If you want to become a comedian you have to have your potential spotted. You can always get it off with turps." Dodd has also made his mark as a singer.

Another giant of the modern era was Eric Morecambe who had fifty different ways to make you laugh and, if all else failed, he produced a paper bag and caught imaginary objects.

In the present decade Joe Pasquale has been a success, especially in Royal Command Galas. He recently stopped the show on the Des O'Connor programme with a toy parrot that wouldn't shut up.

And, of course, there's Mr. Bean, better known as Rowan Atkinson. His television sketch, alone on his birthday in a fancy restaurant, is a classic of choreography, as good as anything Charlie Chaplin achieved. The name of the game was to get rid of a loathsome steak tartare (raw) without anyone noticing. When all his manoeuvres came back to haunt him at the end, he turned it into a triumph of comedy.

His television work was good but, alas, his cinema films, aimed at a very young audience, were disappointing.

Some of the new challengers include Billy Connolly, Paul Merton, Alan Partridge, Rory Bremner, Angus Deayton, Jack Dee and Alan Davies. The great new comedians continue to emerge year after year. Britain is destined to rule the world in the field of comedy for many years to come.

Chapter Two

Champions of Your Century : 1900 – 1999

FEMALE COMEDIANS

Jennifer Saunders carried British humour into new dimensions in the TV series Absolutely Fabulous when she decided to redesign her whole house – or at least buy a more exciting door handle. She'd seen just the thing but couldn't recall where. Then she remembers. She and her pal, Joanna Lumley, take Concorde to New York where Jennifer locates the office building she had been in a long time ago.

When they enter the immense foyer with plush sofas and giant plants, Jennifer says: "That's how I want my kitchen, darling." They rush up the stairs to a small office and Jennifer says triumphantly: "Door handle!"

They take a photo of it and fly home to Britain. Well, redesigning your house is never easy.

The television series was a great career boost for both of them.

Jennifer, of course, was also doing well as part of French and Saunders. Dawn French, meanwhile, thrived in her own career while her partner was off in New York.

As a result, all three of them had become major contenders for the title of the greatest female comedian of the Century.

There were many others.

From the early years there was Dora Bryan, Joyce Grenfell and the all-playing, all-singing Tessie (Two-Ton Tessie) O'Shea.

Gracie Fields became one of the first international female comedy superstars because of her success in films. She was number one in the late Thirties and the early years of the war.

Most comedians followed her example and looked to the cinema or, later, television to make their reputations.

The sitcoms produced stars like Pauline Collins in No, Honestly, Penelope Keith in To The Manor Born, Prunella Scales in Fawlty Towers and Pauline Quirke and Linda Robson as Sharon and Tracy in Birds of a Feather.

The Carry On films gave us the dynamic Barbara Windsor along with Joan Sims and Hattie Jacques.

Other possible candidates from various sources include: Maureen Lipman, Mrs. Merton, Celia Imrie and Bessie Love.

From top: The Vicar of Dibbley – Dawn French (photo courtesy BBC/Tiger Aspect Productions); **Gracie Fields with Sydney Howard in 'Shipyard Sally'.** (1939, 20th Century Fox) (photo courtesy Channel 4); **Victoria Wood in 1993** (photo courtesy BBC); **and Maureen Lipman in 1990.**

**Clockwise from top: Carol Burnett;
Dora Bryan** (Photo from Northcliffe Newspapers, 1987)
**Joyce Grenfell in 1979;
Caroline Ahern as Mrs Merton** (photo courtesy BBC);
Joanna Lumley arriving by helicopter at the Couture hosiery factory, Stoney Stanton, in 1981 (Photo from Leicester Mercury)

There are two challengers from America who need to be considered.

One is Carol Burnett who must certainly hold the record for producing the longest laugh of the Century.

It came in a TV spoof of the film, Gone With the Wind. In the movie, Scarlett O'Hara has gone bankrupt in the American Civil War and she decides to turn to Rhett Butler for help. However, she is reduced to wearing rags. As she looks out the window she tries to think of a way to get some new clothes. Suddenly she notices the curtains and quickly turns them into a beautiful new dress.

In the comedy show, Harvey Kormar playing Rhett waits at the bottom of a long staircase. Carol, as Scarlett, begins her impressive descent, wearing a dress that is lovely except the curtain rod extends from each shoulder, as she has forgotten to remove it.

There is a two-minute laugh, but it's only the beginning.

When Rhett, through the laughter, says the dress is a bit unusual, Carol responds with the classic line: "I saw it in the window and I couldn't resist it!"

The laughter continued for a total of five minutes and, as they say, the joke stopped the show.

The undoubted queen of American comedy was Lucille Ball, who starred in the I Love Lucy television show for several decades.

Her most famous adventure is when she hosts a party at her house for Elizabeth Taylor who will be displaying her new diamond for the first time. For security reasons, the diamond is delivered to Lucy's house for safe-keeping. Inevitably Lucy tries it on, third finger, left hand, and, of course, can't get it off.

When Elizabeth arrives to stand in the receiving line, Lucy hides

And then we come to Victoria Wood, a unique phenomenon of the last twenty years of the Century.

She has continued to be a superstar the way they did it in the old days, as a stand up comedian, working alone. It's true she has been in a number of television shows, often with Julie Walters, but her main occupation is stand-up comic. She's very good and she may be the last of her kind.

These are the main British contenders.

behind a curtain and extends her hand forward as though it was Elizabeth's left hand. All goes well until Richard Burton arrives and admires his wife's ring. Lucy goes wild with excitement and with her hand begins to pat Richard's face. Elizabeth Taylor begins shouting at her left hand to behave.

It ends with the guests watching in astonishment as Elizabeth uses her right hand to pummel her left hand into submission. All very funny stuff.

Lucy is also remembered for her grape stomping skit and the conveyor belt of chocolates moving at high speed while Lucy tries to pack them in boxes. There are so many chocolates moving so fast she is forced to shove some in her pockets or in her mouth in desperation.

There have been many happy hours over the Century from the female comedians on both continents.

Lucille Ball (left) with friend, Vivian Vance, in their popular TV Show.

A Final Interview with Gracie Fields

Gracie Fields was kind enough to grant me an exclusive interview when she was on her farewell concert tour just before she retired.

She wanted to say how heartbroken she was that the newspapers had accused her of being unpatriotic for leaving Britain with her husband in the middle of the war. She had married an Italian and all was well until Italy entered the war on the wrong side.

She was afraid he might be arrested, simply for being Italian, and so they moved away.

Up to that point she had been a beacon of patriotism and hope. Her song, Wish Me Luck As You Wave Me Goodbye, had been the favourite song for departing troops at dockside until it was surpassed by Vera Lynn singing We'll Meet Again.

Gracie had also been the performer who sang what many believe is the ultimate patriotic song, "I'm the girl that makes the thing that holds the oil that oils the ring that works the the thing-ummy-bob that's going to win the war." She said the song was a pledge from all the girls at home to their men in the front lines that they were with them all the way in their fight against the enemy.

"Well," she said, "I hope someday I will be forgiven for whatever it is I'm supposed to have done wrong. Like many other people I fell in love during the war. It was not a convenient time to fall in love; for me or for millions of others. That's the whole story."

I asked her if she had kept a scrapbook of her career and she replied she had started to but then gave it up after the fuss about her leaving during the war. She said that

Gracie Fields, from 'Just Gracie' broadcast on Boxing Day, 1960.
(photo courtesy BBC)

now she was on the eve of retirement she sometimes would take the book out and look at newspaper cuttings from the early years of her career.

I suggested it must give her a sense of pride to have accomplished so much in a short period of time.

She replied, "The truth is, when I look through the book, it is now so long ago that I almost feel that I'm reading about someone else. I have difficulty believing that it was me who did all those things. It's only when I perform at a concert that I am reassured I am still the Gracie Fields I read about in the scrapbook."

A few minutes later we went for a stroll. Suddenly there was a shout from a group of women of uncertain age: "Look! There's our Gricie!"

They came running over to talk to her.

And so it went through the afternoon, recognition and shouts and always with the "rice" sound when they shouted "our Gricie."

She gave me free tickets to the concert.

It was a revelation. As a youngster I had known her only from the radio broadcasts and it was always the comedy. She was always trying to get Walter to the altar and being amazed to see the biggest Aspidistra in the world.

One of my favourite wartime memories was listening to her recitation: What's The Good of a Birthday? I can remember she was warned not to eat too many of the birthday treats because "You can't get sick on your birthday".

She, of course, ate up the lot "and then I showed them if I could get sick or not!"

All a delightful childhood memory.

These comedy routines were all part of the concert. But it was the serious songs, which I was hearing for the first time, that impressed me the most. Gracie Fields had a voice in a very high register and it was absolutely perfect for Sally and her post-war hit, Red Sails In The Sunset.

But I was not prepared for what happened at the finale of her farewell show. She began to sing Ave Maria, higher and higher and higher. I have never heard anyone, anywhere, sing it with such beauty and perfection.

She was one of the great female comedy stars of the first fifty years. She was that and so much more.

Chapter Three
Champions of Your Century : 1900 – 1999
COMEDY TEAMS

The famous comedian Groucho Marx liked to brag about his hunting exploits.

He said: "When I was in Africa, I shot an elephant in my pyjamas. How the elephant got in my pyjamas, I'll never know."

Which is our way of announcing the start of our third major category, the Outstanding Comedy Teams of the Century.

Groucho Marx teamed up with Chico and Harpo to form The Marx Brothers, one of America's most famous comedy groups. They are best known for their Stateroom Scene, when they welcome half the passengers and crew of the ocean liner into their very tiny room.

In Britain, Ronnie Barker said the most popular routine by the Two Ronnies was the one in which he comes into a shop to order a number of items. Ronnie Corbett is the shopkeeper.

Corbett: "You want four candles? Right, here they are. One, two, three, four; four candles."

Barker: "No, not four candles. I want forkhandles; handles for forks."

After five minutes of this, Corbett is in a tailspin.

Corbett: "You want hoes? No? Hose! All right! What kind of hose? Stockings? Garden hose?"

Barker: "No, I'm making a sign. I need letter O's."

Morecambe and Wise were best known for their Christmas shows. In 1977 about half the population of Britain watched their Yule programme.

Some of their famous routines included the time Shirley Bassey lost a shoe while on stage singing Smoke Gets In Your Eyes. Morecambe and Wise try to put a shoe on her bare foot without anyone noticing.

A routine with Morecambe playing piano for an orchestra conducted by a very game Andre Previn is also highly memorable.

When Previn accuses him of playing the wrong notes, Eric is quick to correct him.

"I'm playing the right notes – but not necessarily in the right order!"

From America, Bud Abbott and Lou Costello became candidates for the best comedy team of the Century on the basis of this routine, called Who's On First.

You don't have to know anything about baseball to enjoy the fast-moving play on words.

Top: The Two Ronnies – Corbett and Barker on Christmas Night 1987 (photo courtesy BBC);
Middle: Harry Secombe, Spike Milligan and Michael Bentine three of the Goons, at a 1991 re-union (the absent member of the team was Peter Sellers);
Bottom: The Marx Brothers – Chico, Groucho and Harpo in *A Night in Casablanca* (1946, United Artists. photo courtesy BBC).

left: **Bud Abbott and Lou Costello, in 'Jack and The Beanstalk' in 1965.** (photo courtesy BBC)
Below left: Laurel and Hardy getting into another fine mess.

Right from Top: The team from Black Adder II (photo courtesy BBC, 1985)**; Flanagan and Allen in 1953; The Crazy Gang in 1962** (photo courtesy ATV)**; John Cleese in Fawlty Towers** (photo courtesy BBC)**; French and Saunders in 1987** (photo courtesy BBC).

Abbott: "Baseball players these days have some very strange names, like Dizzy Dean. I discovered this because I now own a team."

Costello: "Are they any good?"

Abbott: "They're very good."

Costello: "Who's your first baseman?"

Abbott: "Yes."

Costello: "I want to know, Who's on first?"

Abbott: "That's right."

Costello: "I want to know his name. At the end of the week, when you pay the first baseman, Who gets the money?"

Abbott: "Every penny of it!"

Costello: "You have a second baseman? What's his name?"

Abbott: "That's right."

Costello: "Who's on second?"

Abbott: "No, Who's on first."

Costello: "Who's on first? What's his name?"

Clockwise from top: The Monty Python Team – back row: Graham Chapman, Eric Idle and Terry Gilliam; front row: Terry Jones, John Cleese and Michael Palin. (photo courtesy BBC.); **Morecambe and Wise enjoy a 1988 Christmas show with Glenda Jackson;** (photo courtesy BBC); **Dawson and Friends – Les Dawson joins the Turnip People in 1977** (photo courtesy Yorkshire Television)

Below Roy Castle, on a visit to Leicester in 1987. (Photo from Leicester Mercury)

Abbott: "What's on second."
Costello: "Who's on second?"
Abbott: "First base!!"

Possibly even more famous are the comedy team of Laurel and Hardy, made up of Stan Laurel from Britain and Oliver Hardy from America. They specialised in sight comedy gags.

In the middle of the century Flanagan and Allen were well liked and The Crazy Gang had many fans, including, it was said, The Queen Mother.

More recent comedy teams in Britain include Hale and Pace, Cannon and Ball, Little and Large and many more. Other American comedy teams that could be considered include Gallagher and Shean from the 1930s, along with George Burns and Gracie Allen, Dean Martin and Jerry Lewis and a number of trios patterned after The Marx Brothers.

The British-born comedian, Bob Hope, teamed up with American Bing Crosby for ten years to make the highly-successful Road Films.

Here in Britain many people will remember this brilliant routine from 1962 by Roy Castle, Jimmy James and Eli Woods.

Roy walks in with a small box under his arm and announces he has just returned from a holiday in South Africa where they gave him a present of two man-eating lions.

Jimmy asks: "Did you fetch them home?"
Roy: "Yes."
Jimmy: "Where are they?"
Roy: "They're in the box."

It turns out Roy had also visited Nyasaland where they gave him a giraffe.

Jimmy: "They would. They're nice people the Nyasas. Where is the giraffe?"
Roy: "It's in the box."

Roy also went to India where they gave him an elephant. Jimmy asks if the elephant is in the box and

Roy replies: "Don't be silly, you couldn't get an elephant in the box."

Eli suggests: "You could ask the giraffe to move over."

It turns out the elephant is in a cage. Jimmy asks, "Where's the cage?"

Roy: "It's in the box!"

Candidates for the greatest comedy team of the Century also include many of the famous radio and television shows.

Some of the best are the Fawlty Towers team of John Cleese, Prunella Scales, Andrew Sachs and Connie Booth along with French and Saunders, and The Goon Show. Also highly regarded is Monty Python, featuring the late Graham Chapman of Leicester

Best Comedians: What You Said

Here is what you had to say on the categories of the Best Comedy Teams and Best Male and Female Comedians of the Century.

Pat Middleton of Braunstone Town nominates Victoria Wood as top female comic "she is so down to earth with no airs or graces" with Maureen Lipman in second place, "another lady who is so good at everything she does."

As for the best comedy teams: "It's got to be Morecambe and Wise, they are family fun for all ages." In second place are: "French and Saunders, these are two ladies who can do anything; they complement each other."

Mr. G. Betts of Ibstock writes: "My choice for the best comedy team without any doubt is Laurel and Hardy.

"Ever since I was young I've enjoyed watching the boys and never tire of seeing their films. Their timeless humour is as popular now as it ever was. They will never be forgotten."

Dennis Stevenson of Melton Mowbray writes: "The top female comedian has to be Victoria Wood. She has brought an entirely new formula for comedy and her presentation is second to none."

He continues, "The Greatest Comedy Team of the Century is Morecambe and Wise. They didn't have to say anything to get the audience ready to explode with mirth. This was the gift they had. It made them stand above any other comedy team.

"The Two Ronnies ran them a close second."

Les Dawson was a very popular comedian, by himself and also in a team with Roy Barraclough, both dressed as thirty-something women. In one of their best routines, Ms. Les admits that 'she' is approaching the Change.

Roy replies: "Approaching the Change? From which direction?"

Ian Morton of Leicester also writes to praise Les Dawson.

"He was a wonderful stand-up comic who came out with witty one-liners and good characterisations such as Cosmo Smallpiece or as one of the seaside landladies with Roy Barraclough.

Left: Hancock's Half Hour – Tony Hancock as a reluctant blood donor (photo courtesy BBC).

Right: Ken Dodd risks a tickling from three Hinckley children in 1883. (Photo from Leicester Mercury)

"One of his best jokes was: My wife is so unfetching, when she went for a swim in Loch Ness, the Monster got out and picketed the Loch!"

T.J. Langham of Hinckley writes: "I've always appreciated Les Dawson over many years.

"One joke I remember was when he said that as a small boy the family were so poor that the mice used to bring them scraps."

"A particular favourite of mine was Nat Mills and Bobbie, husband and wife, with the catch phrase, Let's get on with it!"

"And, finally, there was Old Mother Riley and Kitty (Lucan and McShane)."

"I used to live at Burbage and loved going to the variety shows at Coventry Hippodrome."

Dennis J. Duggan of Leicester contributes two jokes by one of his favourite comedians, George Roper.

At a council meeting the Mayor put forward a plan for a safari park in a tough area of his city.

"Hang on," said a councillor, "What if the lions and tigers escape?"

The Mayor replied: "Then the lions and tigers would have to take their chances like the rest of us!"

In the same city the dustmen went on strike at Christmas. George Roper said the citizens got rid of their rubbish by wrapping it in Christmas paper and leaving it on the back seat of their car.

Nigel Hanwell of Barwell, Leicester, writes to vote for Freddie Frinton. "This man is a comic genius when it comes to portraying drunks. Every year his Dinner for One show is shown on television on New Years Eve."

Doug V. Pither of Leicester Forest East writes to support Gracie Fields as one of the best female comedians. "She was a great star and also very popular in films and a major recording artist."

"For best comedy teams how about Collinson & Breen, one very short and the other very tall in army uniforms. The short one used to say, 'Everyone put up their plates for treacle and somebody pinched mine!"

"I also remember the Cockney kids, Ethel Revnell and Gracie West, and the popular Americans, Bebe Daniels and Ben Lyon with children Barbara and adopted son Richard in Life With The Lyons."

He also voted for Suzette Tarri, "a major variety and radio performer" and also for Jeanne De Casalis, "her whole comedy act was spent on a telephone."

Brian Manship of Leicester votes for Peter Sellers, Walter Matthau, Tony Hancock, Phil Silvers and Ken Dodd in the category of Best Male Comedian. He supports Victoria Wood, Margarate Rutherford, Dawn French, Joyce Grenfell and Beryl Read for Best Female Comedian.

For Outstanding Comedy Team he votes for Laurel and Hardy, Walter Matthau and Jack Lemmon from The Odd Couple, The Goons, Morecambe and Wise and George Burns and Gracie Allen.

L.E. Mattock of Leicester votes for: Frankie Howerd, Max Wall, Max Miller, George Formby and Bob Monkhouse.

D. Neate of Glen Parva supports: Max Miller, John Cleese, Max Wall, and Tommy Trinder for Male Comedian and Laurel and Hardy for Top Comedy Team and also Lucille Ball, Prunella Scales, Victoria Wood, Barbara Windsor and Jennifer Saunders for Best Female Comedy Star.

Derek Foster of Leicester votes for Laurel and Hardy as Best Comedy Team and Dave Allen and Jasper Carrott in the category of Top Male Comedians.

M.D. Matts of Wigston votes for: Frankie Howerd, Ken Dodd, Arthur Askey, Norman Wisdom and Charlie Chaplin.

T. Fish of Melton Mowbray writes: "After due thought I have to nominate these for the title of Comedy Star of the Century: Benny Hill, Tommy Cooper, Ken Dodd and Les Dawson."

Joy Lynes of Kibworth selects Max Miller as the King of Comedy. "I met him each time he came to the

From top: **Bob Monkhouse presents 'Bob's Christmas Full House' for 1985.** (photo courtesy BBC)**; Benny Hill; Nicholas Parsons visits the Charnwood Theatre for a recording of Just a Minute, in 1997; George Formby, in search of a certain little lady; Phil Silvers as Sergeant Bilko** (photo courtesy BBC)

Leicester Palace. My other selections are Les Dawson, Bob Hope, George Formby and, for comedy team, Eric Morecambe and Ernie Wise."

Roy Tilly of Leicester votes for Wally Bosworth as the best Leicester Comedian.

Doug V. Pither of Leicester Forest East writes: "My first choice is Tommy Cooper. He was brilliant. He never cracked jokes, you only had to look at his face. How we miss him. Second is Norman Evans, dressed as a woman in Over the Garden Wall.

Third is Tony Hancock, so brilliant on the radio and TV. I loved The Blood Donor.

Fourth, Michael Barrymore, so polished in all that he does and fifth Nat (Rubber Neck) Jackley, very tall and hilarious when he did the Soldiers on Parade sketch.

Best Female Comedian is Dawn French from Vicar of Dibley and Best Comedy Team is Morecambe and Wise."

P. Gargan of Leicester writes: "I have to vote for Ken Dodd, Ken Dodd, Ken Dodd, Ken Dodd and Ken Dodd. My favourite routine is when he says if you are in a strange hotel and you wake up in the middle of the night and you want to know the time, bang a drum outside the window. Someone is bound to shout: 'Who the heck is banging a drum at four o'clock in the morning?!"

Dennis Stevenson of Melton Mowbray votes for Benny Hill, Les Dawson, Tommy Cooper, Ronnie Barker and an Irish comedian, Hal Roach.

Dennis J. Duggan of Leicester votes for Top Male Comedian: Rowan Atkinson (No. 1), Stanley Baxter, Harry Worth, Roy Barraclough, Les Dawson. Top Female Comedian: Victoria Wood (No. 1), Dawn French, Joyce Grenfell, Prunella Scales, Barbara Windsor. Top Comedy Team: Laurel & Hardy (No. 1), French & Saunders, The Two Ronnies, Les Dawson & Roy Barraclough and Little & Large.

Stephanie Duggan of Leicester votes for Top Male Comedian: Ronnie Barker (No. 1), Dave Allen, Rowan Atkinson, Terry Scott, Jasper Carrott. Top Female Comedian: Joyce Grenfell (No. 1), Victoria Wood, Dawn French. Top Comedy Team: The Two Ronnies (No. 1) Morecambe & Wise, French & Saunders, Monty Python and Little & Large.

Philip Marshall of Syston writes: "My top comedian is John Cleese. Surprisingly, no folk seem to mention Arthur Haynet. He was brilliant in his time. With Nicholas Parsons, he was the funniest man on tele!"

From top:
Prunella Scales in 1990 (Photo: Leicester Mercury.)
Jennifer Saunders in 1994 (photo courtesy BBC.)
Penelope Keith in 1995 (Photo by Chris Capstick from BBC Radio 4 – 'My Kind of Trust'.)
Right: The Two Ronnies in 1985 (photo courtesy BBC)

Chapter Four
Champions of Your Century : 1900 – 1999
BREEDS OF DOG

Above: Labrador puppies
Below: Clockwise from top left – a King Charles Spaniel; Rodders the Great Dane with tiny pal, Sunny, from Sharnford; Cocker Spaniel, Colinwood Silver Lariot; and Xolochi, the Mexican Hairless, from Barlestone. (Photos from Leicester Mercury)

When your troubles almost overwhelm you, it's nice to know you have a friend with a cold nose and a waggily tail. You will always be greeted with a smile.

One of our most delightful categories was the search for the people's favourite breed of dog of the Century.

Dogs are the centre of so many wonderful anecdotes.

For example, I will always remember the newspaper account of Sam, a Border Collie, walking in the park with his elderly master. The man placed a blanket on the grass so they could sit down and rest.

The man suddenly took ill. He struggled to his feet, told his dog "stay!" and then staggered into town where he collapsed and was rushed to hospital.

Three days later, when he came to, he asked his family to make sure his dog was all right. It took a full day of searching before they discovered where he was. They found Sam still lying on the blanket in the park.

They tried to get the dog to come home but he wouldn't move except, every ten minutes, he would stand up, gaze into the distance and then lie down again, whining.

He refused to leave the blanket, even when offered food.

Hearing about this, the old man insisted upon being released from hospital, and, with the help of his family, managed to reach his dog, still lying on the blanket in the park. Seeing his master, Sam leapt up and danced around him happily. The man was ill, the dog was starving but none of that seemed to matter. They were both deliriously happy.

The newspaper account had the heading: The Dog That Was Told To Stay.

Another newspaper report that lingers in the mind involves a man who founded a successful company but now, at 70, he is voted out of office by the younger members of his board who have plans to modernise the business. The first decision of the new management is to get rid of Fred, the elderly German Shepherd dog who has spent most of his life guarding the company safe. He is replaced by two young and snarling dogs of a fiercer breed.

Two days later, for the first time in the history of the company, the safe is robbed. Near the safe are the bones left over from the raw steak the burglars gave the two dogs to keep them quiet.

Told about this, the old man was not surprised. "Many dogs are far more fierce than Fred. But the German Shepherd has a characteristic that is very rare. He can not be bought off. He is absolutely incorruptible."

To me, that is the most wonderful thing that can be said about a dog or a person. Here is someone you can trust absolutely, a true friend.

The third anecdote is so amazing that I wouldn't have believed it if I hadn't seen it for myself.

I was standing on a small pier at a lake when I suddenly heard a loud whistle from a man in a rowboat. Out of nowhere a Spaniel came roaring down the pier and jumped into the water.

The dog began swimming back and forth, apparently going nowhere, making great splashes.

I became concerned and asked a bystander about it.

"Don't worry," he said. "That's just Sally."

"But she must be almost exhausted. Shouldn't I dive in and rescue her?"

"No. You don't have to worry about Sally. She's a fish dog."

"A what?"

"A fish dog. Watch!"

Now she was splashing closer and closer to the rowboat. The man put his fishing line into the water and started pulling out trout, one after the other.

"You see? Sally is herding the fish for him."

"Herding the fish?"

He shrugged. "Of course. She does it all the time. She's rather good at it."

Which all goes to prove, when it comes to dogs, you can learn something new every day.

This category turned out to be the most popular by far and I was soon up to my knees in letters. It got so busy that one night I dreamt about dogs. Over the hill they came, more than thirty of the cutest puppies you ever saw, all wagging their tails and carrying letters in their mouth.

It was a shame to have to wake up and get back to work.

From top: Scraggy, the faithful mongrel; Malcolm, Harley, Bridget and Mr Smith, four Dachshunds from Thurcaston; a Labrador; Cindy, an Old English Sheepdog, with friend Gemma; and an English Springer Spaniel. (Photos from Leicester Mercury)

Dogs: What You Said

Mrs. D. Coupe, Kibworth, Leicester: "My favourite breed is the Border Collie.

"It is loving, obedient, faithful, extremely intelligent (including telepathy) easily trained, a good house guard.

"Medium sized and beautifully marked. It looks like a dog should look. What more could one ask?

"Other favourite breeds are Alsatian, Labrador, Golden Retriever, Husky."

Mrs. B. Connolly of Braunstone, Leicester: "My favourite breeds of dogs are the Alsatian, Lurcher, Yorkshire Terrier, Great Dane, St. Bernard, Springer Spaniel, Labrador and a Retriever."

Alison Ladkin, 15, of Markfield, Leicester: "My first dog was a yellow Labrador and believe it or not her name was 'Leicester' as we support the Leicester City F.C. She would eat absolutely anything and, once when we gave her a piece of onion, she ate it so quick and, afterwards, made such a funny face as though to say 'that was disgusting'.

"She did not like hot air balloons and always barked at them. Also, even though she was meant to be a hunting dog, if she saw a dead animal then she would stand next to it and cry!

"My second favourite dog is the German Shepherd. I love those dogs so much! Tess has only just turned one and all she ever wants to do is play. It doesn't matter what you throw for her, she will still go and fetch it. Even though she is a real softie, if there is anybody knocking on the door or a noise outside then she will bark very deeply. Once we were watching TV and the TV police smashed a window and Tess wouldn't stop barking!

"I also love the look of the Siberian Husky. They look so pretty but also look quite aggressive at the same time.

"I also love Pugs as they have a great character and a lovely but very funny look on their face. I have not ever seen a Whippet but I have been told that they are lovely dogs and very affectionate towards their master."

An unsigned letter from Fallowfield Road, Leicestershire: "My first choice is the Border Collie. My second choice is a Yorkshire Terrier."

Linda Taylor of Atherstone, Warwickshire: "My favourite breed of dog is the smooth-haired Fox Terrier.

"They are lovely, lively, happy dogs, full of fun and life. They are a guard and a pal and they will even catch you a dinner if you fancy a rabbit.

"They are good house dogs, clowns and very, very faithful.

"My first Fox Terrier, Pedro, lived to be 14 but he was hit by an ambulance. It hurt very deeply. Now I have four of them, black and white. The mother is 17, the dad is 10 and there are two daughters, both eight.

"I love all dogs but my vote is for the Fox Terrier."

Carmen, 9, of Leicestershire: "I have been thinking about voting for my favourite dogs and I like the Husky, Rough Collie, English Sheepdog, Corgi, St. Bernard and white West Highland Terrier."

Mrs. Osborne of Market Harborough: "My favourite breed is the German Shepherd but would love to have another dog that would live to be a bit older as mine died when it was 13. I have taken an English Spaniel as it is stronger than a German Shepherd."

Mrs. C. Jane of Abbey Rise, Leicester: "My favourite breed of dog is the Rough Collie. They are faithful, elegant, always turn people's heads with their beautiful looks.

Monique Scott's two Huskies enjoying some winter weather at Beacon Hill, Leicestershire. (Photo from Leicester Mercury)

"They can sometimes be a bit noisy but with their loving faces you soon forgive them. I have had two Collies and also a German Shepherd, which is very well known for intelligence, stamina and charm.

"My other favourite dogs are Labradors, boisterous; King Charles Spaniel for the waggiest tail; Dachshund, sweet; Tibetan Spaniel, cute; Doberman, faithful; Golden Retriever, clever.

"And please don't forget the faithful mongrel."

Hannah Clarke, age 10, of Glenfield: "My favourite breed is the Golden Retriever. Others I also like are the Longhaired Dachshund, West Highland Terrier, American Cocker Spaniel, Labrador and Beagle."

Mrs. G. Astley of Leicestershire: "My favourite breed of dog is the Belgian Shepherd. They are very loyal and obedient and make excellent guard dogs.

"I also like Corgis as they have similar qualities."

Mrs. F. Cynthia Tolkan of Leicester: "Some years ago I would certainly have put at the top of my list of favourite breeds: German Shepherds, large Poodles, Border Collies and Cairns.

"However, an incident one year ago put a different breed at the very top of my list.

It happened when I was waiting for as train at a foreign railway station. Two magnificent dogs were tethered to a post on the platform, their owners being only a short distance away.

"I could hardly believe my eyes. These beautiful animals were almost the size of ponies.

"I asked the owners if it was all right to stroke them. That was the wonderful moment when I made the acquaintance of two Irish Wolfhounds. I used both my free hands, one for each nuzzling head.

"Those friendly eyes, their splendid coats of long grey hair, their patient insistence that I should continue to make a fuss over them.

"Oh, yes, I was a devotee for life.

"I hope to hear of any local Irish Wolfhounds and have the chance to meet them."

Miss J. Sewell of Scraptoft: "My favourite breed is the Border Collie. Ours came from Animal Aid when he was one and he instantly became a member of the family.

He is twelve now but is still as loving as ever and is always alert when callers arrive who he does not recognise.

I am also fond of the English Setter and the German Shepherd but in our house there is only one favourite dog, our Border Collie."

Suzanne Gibson of Coalville: "My favourite breed is the Boxer, who, if

**Left: An Irish Wolfhound.
Right, from top: A St Bernard named Spot befriends Topsy the Cairn terrier; Pillerton Peterton, a West Highland Terrier; an Italian Greyhound; Beattie the Beagle; Cindy, a German Shepherd Dog with Mark Brooks; a Bassett Hound; a Collie; and a Jack Russell.** (Photos from Leicester Mercury)

allowed, will become the largest lap dog I know. Full of character, he is a reliable and trusty friend for life.

His aim is to be a member of the family. He craves human affection and will defend his loved ones, although, in a quiet way, he prefers to stay with children as playmate and protector.

He is always alert to a strange noise but will not bark without cause. He is perceptive, especially of his owners. During a recent illness on a couple of occasions I was unable to take him for a walk. He did not ask once. He just lay beside me all day, snuffling against my face every now and then, as if to check that I was okay.

One word of warning for any prospective Boxer owner, insure him as they are very accident prone and, certainly for the first couple of years, they will charge headlong into any danger because they are fearless."

Elaine Andrea Hicklin of Beaumont Leys: "As a child I had a Golden Cocker Spaniel (English) and in my teens I had a Cardigan Corgi. Now I have one Yorkshire Terrier and three Crossbreeds/ Mongrels.

I have found the Crossbreeds to be the best. They are loyal, easy to train and hardy in health. I have found the Yorkshire Terrier to suffer several health problems. The most robust of my pedigrees I have had has been the Cardigan Corgi, so this is my preferred choice of the pedigree dogs."

Andria Robertson, 13, of Leicester: "My favourite dog is the longhaired miniature Dachshund and I have three who patrol the neighbourhood with their loud bark. They are not a little 'toy' dog that topples over when the wind blows. They are strong, loving, affectionate and, if there is an intruder and their bark is heard, they can sound quite dangerous!"

Louise Roberts of Syston: "Delighted to see a photograph of the mini long-hair Dachshund. I owned my first mini smooth Dachshund in 1941 and in 1954 I bought my first mini wirehaired Dachshund and bred from her. I love all types of this breed and my favourites are the mini wires; so bravely courageous and wonderful pets, hunters and guard dogs."

The final four votes to arrive in time to be counted were from Mrs. D. G. Woodford of Leicester, D. W. Protheroe of Leicester, Lynn Tipton of Barwell, Leicester, and from a young Shitsu named Baby 'Legend' Taylor, of Anstey Lane, Leicester.

Thank you for all your interesting letters.

Top: A well spotted Dalmatian.
Left: Ooer – A Dachshund gets a bit of a shock when a Deerhound says hello. (Photos from Leicester Mercury)

Chapter Five
Champions of Your Century : 1900 – 1999

WAR SONGS

It was the great songs that helped us get through the wars of this Century. Glenn Miller was playing In The Mood for soldiers in an outdoor concert in the south of England when the audience was scattered by a sudden air raid.

Those first back on their feet were the musicians and they resumed the song despite the continuing explosions not far away.

Hearing the music the soldiers got back to their feet cheering and singing with defiance at the enemy. Those who were there will never forget the moment.

Our question today is: What are your favourite songs from the war years and what memories do the songs have for you?

The candidates are in two types: those specifically about the war and those that may simply be love ballads or dance tunes but bring back vivid memories of the war years.

For example, my uncle in Canada was sitting in a pub in Halifax, looking at a sign on the wall, Loose Lips Sink Ships, and hoping no enemy submarine commander knew he would soon be boarding a troopship bound for Britain. If he was going to become a casualty he at least wanted the chance to arrive safely in England.

To forget his worries he was having a beer and telling jokes with his buddies and paying no attention

**From top: Militiamen queue up for rations at the Glen Parva Depot;
Members of the Women's Land Army in 1944;
Checking the stirrup pumps and other fire-fighting equipment;
Mr & Mrs Shelley in 1941, who "showed their contempt for the Nazis by putting out the Union Jack after their home had been bombed."** (Photos from Leicester Mercury)

Top left: **Allocation of gasmasks at Catherine Street School at the start of the second world war;**
Top right: **The Home Guard, at drill duties;**
Centre: **Troops take time out to pursue hobbies, such as constructing a model of a landscape.** (Photos from Leicester Mercury)

to the jukebox. Suddenly he became aware of the voice of Frank Sinatra singing Long Ago and Far Away. My uncle couldn't stop the tears. He had just come across Canada on a train. Long ago was last week. Far Away was 5,000 miles. Only five days had passed but now it seemed that his wife and children had all been in a previous lifetime and he wasn't sure if he would ever see them again.

He fought in Europe and survived. Despite all the fighting, his most vivid memory of the war was that moment in a pub in Halifax when Frank Sinatra sang Long Ago and Far Away.

Here, the war got under way with Gracie Fields cheerfully singing, Wish Me Luck As You Wave Me Goodbye. This soon would change to Vera Lynn singing the more sombre, We'll Meet Again.

Similarly, America entered the war with the light-hearted tune, Praise The Lord and Pass The Ammunition. However, before long everyone was humming Coming In On A Wing and a Prayer. Earlier, Bette Davis had a bit of fun with They're Either Too Young or Too Old, but then later Dinah Shore was singing the melancholy hit, I'll Walk Alone.

I was a young lad during the war and one of my most vivid memories was sitting in a classroom singing The White Cliffs of Dover. I was greatly moved by the words:

"And Jimmy will go to sleep
In his own little room again."

I can also remember being at a gathering of adults and we were singing I'll Be Seeing You. There were two women beside me, one whose husband was fighting in the Pacific and the other who had already been informed her husband would not be coming back. I'll never forget the moment they came to the final two lines of the song:

"I'll be looking at the moon
But I'll be seeing you."

The First World War was a long time ago but the songs are still with us. The first two that come to mind are It's A Long Way To Tipperary and Pack Up Your Troubles In Your Old Kit Bag and Smile, Smile, Smile.

In America, George M. Cohan contributed, Over There, which had a mixed reception over here.

There were other songs from other wars including the Boer War, which ended in 1902, and the battles since 1945, including Korea, Vietnam, The Falklands, Desert Storm and Kosovo.

War Songs: What You Said

K Lynch of Glenfield: "My favourite songs from the war years are Leaning on a Lamp Post by George Formby, Run Rabbit Run by Flannagan and Allen, In The Mood by Glenn Miller plus several songs by Gracie Fields."

Jean Reilly of Leicester: "A song that should be mentioned is Coming in on a Wing and a Prayer. I also liked As Time Goes By and In The Mood. It has been interesting reading about the old songs. They bring back memories."

Mrs. I Palmer, Melton Mowbray: "Two of my favourite war-time songs were Goodnight Sweetheart and Who's Taking You Home Tonight, which were always played at the end of the dance.

"Two others for obvious reasons, as we lived in the middle of several airfields, were Silver Wings in the Moonlight and Coming in on a Wing and a Prayer. We would watch the bombers going out at night and listen for them coming home.

"We used to go to Woolworths and buy a paper booklet with all the songs in; not music, just the words. They were all beautiful songs with a meaning."

Mrs. E. Childs of Wigston: "For me, Yours will always be my favourite but so many others spring to mind. These include When the Poppies Bloom Again and I Haven't Said Thanks for that Lovely Weekend.

"The words those days meant a lot to us young wives with our men away at war."

Bill Kinton of Leicester: "My favourites are: When Father Papered the Parlour, Little Stick of Blackpool Rock, Lay Down Your Arms, Stage Door Canteen and Chocolate Soldier."

From 3040911 Gray. 'Dolly'. RAF of Leicester: "There are so many songs that bring back memories. One heard them and danced to them.

"I had a girlfriend and my favourite song was I Never Said Thanks for that Lovely Weekend which was very appropriate as I have not seen the girl since.

"I could have been in Room 504 or whistling to A Nightingale Sang in Berkeley Square; however it was A Lovely Day Tomorrow followed by The Way You Look Tonight.

"Who can forget Warsaw Concerto, London Fantasy, Col. Bogey, Ave Maria and Moonlight Serenade?

Gracie Fields, with the Biggest Aspidistra In The World. (photo courtesy BBC, 1937)

"Went on a Lambeth Walk to the Teddy Bears Picnic and met up with Albert The Lion. Finally was Underneath the Arches with Wink Martindale, Deck of Cards and ended up with I'll Walk Alone and Lay Down Your Arms."

Geoff Cooke of Leicester is a fan of the Glenn Miller Band and his favourite songs of the war years include I Know Why, Moonlight Cocktail and Serenade In Blue.

He said his research shows that Miller disbanded his civilian orchestra in September, 1942, and joined the services the following month.

"He did basic training and attended officer school; then he started to recruit for his proposed Army Air Force Band. The Dance Band section included a few of his own musicians. The rest came from the other leading American big bands.

"So the orchestra was actually formed by Glenn Miller. It had a varied repertoire but the classical pieces were generally the 'old' part of the Something Old, Something New, Something Borrowed and Something Blue medleys that were a feature of the band's wartime concerts and broadcasts."

Brian Simpson of Burbage: "I write to say how interesting I find your write-ups on songs of the war years.

"There should be no doubt that at the top or very near the top of the English charts will be The White Cliffs of Dover and We'll Meet Again.

"Both songs were written by the song-writing team of Ross Parker and Hugh Charles who wrote many others, including The Girl in the Alice Blue Gown.

"Unfortunately, one of their other songs made the mistake of being published at the same time as Jimmy Kennedy's hit song We're Going to Hang Out the Washing on the Siegfried Line. Theirs was titled I'm Sending You the Siegfried Line to Hang Your Washing On.

"Kennedy's version went on to be a hit but their Seigfried sank without a trace. (Well, not quite. I have a copy!)"

There were hundreds more letters, unfortunately too many to print.

The four songs your letters mentioned most frequently from the First World War are:

It's a Long Way To Tipperary and Pack Up Your Troubles In Your Old Kit Bag and Smile, Smile, Smile along with Lili Marlene from Germany and Over There from America.

When it came to the Second World War, there were hundreds of favourites.

Because of the large number of American servicemen stationed here after 1941, many of the songs are from across the Atlantic.

These include: I'll Be Seeing You, I'll Walk Alone, Long Ago and Far Away, I'll Never Smile Again and the two great songs from the cinema: You'll Never Know from Hello, Frisco, Hello and As Time Goes By from Casablanca.

In this country, besides The White Cliffs of Dover and We'll Meet Again, we were singing: Roll Out The Barrel, When the Lights Go On Again, A Nightingale Sang in Berkeley Square, We're Going to Get Lit Up When the Lights Go On in London along with George Formby singing The Maginot Line.

Gracie Fields contributed The Biggest Aspidistra In The World with the wartime change of lyrics to:

"We're going to string old Hitler from the very highest bough
of the Biggest Aspidistra in the World."

There were also general songs everyone was humming at the time like Underneath The Arches and Run, Rabbit, Run.

The biggest band influence of the Second World War was Glenn Miller who was a hit everywhere in Britain. But what was his outstanding song? His top tunes included Serenade in Blue, In The Mood, Little Brown Jug, Chattanooga Choo Choo and Pennsylvania 6-5000.

We'll Meet Again by Vera Lynn is a favourite of T.P. Blaney of Leicester, along with songs reflecting his Scottish heritage, including Keep Right On To The End of the Road, It's Twelve and a Tanner a Bottle That's All That It's Costing Tay Day plus Joseph Lock, Hear My Song, and Arthur Tracy, The Street Singer. As a poet he writes under the name of Scotch Tommy and has had a number of his works accepted by the Imperial War Museum. His most recent poem is a tribute to Princess Diana.

Favourites of Mrs. B. Blaney: Sally and Sing As We Go by Gracie Fields, Leaning On a Lamp Post by George Formby, We'll Meet Again and The White Cliffs of Dover by Vera Lynn and String of Pearls and Little Brown Jug by Glenn Miller.

Mrs. L. Vickers: "The songs of Vera Lynn were my favourite."

Walter Malkin of Braunstone was stationed in southern Italy during the war, arriving there at Christmas, 1943. "We were entertained in person by Marlene Dietrich who sang her famous See What the Boys in the Backroom Will Have and the event is still fresh in my mind.

"But the song I know was always with us at that time is You'll Never Know, sung by Alice Faye. It certainly matched the emotion of the time. And, of course, there was Judy Garland with The Trolley Song and so many more."

Arthur Bassett of Leicester: "The number one song of World War Two has got to be The White Cliffs of Dover. As a child I was awakened night after night and taken to the Anderson Shelter next door. I didn't mind because they had a lovely dog called Jill and their daughter Joan had a most infectious laugh (I can still hear it now) and they had a gramophone and records. My mother said I used to sing along with Oh, Johnny, Oh, Johnny, Oh! (I have since found a copy sung by Elsie Carlisle and it brings a lump to my throat and makes my eyes moist).

Leicestershire Soldiers and Sailors grateful to be returning home at the end of World War One, in 1918. (Photos from Leicester Mercury)

"Other favourites include Kiss Me Goodnight Sergeant Major, Bless 'Em All, and Wish Me Luck As You Wave Me Goodbye.

"From 1942 Bing Crosby sang White Christmas. I have memories of noses flattened against Lewis's festively decorated windows and six pence to see Father Christmas. After Father Christmas, into High Street, get some hot chestnuts from the machine and catch a tram up Narborough Road.

"Other favourite songs of the time were Roll Out The Barrel, Lili Marlene and Dance With a Dolly with a Hole in Her Stocking, which has been in my head for fifty odd years."

The final letter to arrive just before this category closed was from J. Edward Hall of Glenfield who points out that isolated in the Mediterranean, there was not a large choice of songs available.

"When we were living in goat pens in Malta, waiting to go to Sicily, the local cinema only had a recording of Amapola (my pretty little poppy) and it was playing as you went in, during any interval, when you came out – and during the many times when the film broke."

Mainly the members of the squadron kept up their spirits by writing their own lyrics to Lili Marlene."

Above: Glenn Miller
Right: George Formby

Chapter Six
Champions of Your Century : 1900 – 1999
ROCK GROUPS

The worst prediction of the century came in 1955 when an American music critic wrote: "As for this latest teenage fad, Rock 'n' Roll, it won't last a year." Some fad! Some year! A few months later, Bill Haley and his Comets brought Rock Around the Clock to Europe and a New Age had begun. American Rock music ruled the world.

However, in 1963, The Beatles captured the hearts of young Europeans with She Loves You and, in 1964, they returned the favour by conquering America with I Want To Hold Your Hand, launching the British Invasion.

It was a wonderful time to be young man in California and have a British accent. All you had to say was: "Oh, yes, I'm British. From Liverpool, actually," and the girls would squeal and crowd around, hoping for a date.

Hundreds of British bands bought airline tickets for America to cash in on the success of The Beatles and many did very well, notably The Rolling Stones in 1965 when Mick Jagger told the whole English-speaking world, I Can't Get No Satisfaction.

The Beatles continued to be the driving force throughout the 1960s with Hey Jude, Help!, Can't Buy Me Love and A Hard Day's Night, along with all the hit songs from Sgt. Pepper's Lonely Hearts Club Band in 1967.

Rock grew in strength in the 1970s and beyond. It would be hazardous to try to capture the full list of the best bands because there were thousands and thousands.

The problem is always to separate the fabulous bands like The Who, Simply Red, Police, Fleetwood Mac, Blondie, U2 and Doors from those that were so great they ruled the world like Queen, The Beatles, ABBA and The Bee Gees.

We knew from the start it would be a difficult task to find the top ten finalists.

First of all, it was important to side-step the argument about how to define Rock music. The debate could take over a thousand years to resolve. Quite simply, we use Rock in the only practical way, in its widest sense to include Punk, Heavy Metal, Pop and all other variations of what could be called the music of

From top: Oasis (photo courtesy Creation Records)**;**
Aerosmith;
Bon Jovi in 1985;
The Beach Boys (photo courtesy EMI Records UK)

the young people, but of course much of it is enjoyed by almost everyone.

Here is a small sampling of some of the bands from the history of Rock.

Velvet Underground, U2, R.E.M., Sex Pistols, Led Zeppelin, The Band, Clash, Doors,

Dire Straits, Simple Minds, Meat Loaf, Blondie, Steely Dan, Deep Purple, Oasis, Eurythmics, Bon Jovi, Jefferson Airplane, Byrds, Yes, Supertramp, Eagles, Wham!, Take That, Boys Zone, UB40, Foreigner, Wet Wet Wet, Blood Sweat and Tears and Kiss.

There are hundreds more great bands including AC/DC, Aerosmith, Rush, Earth Wind & Fire, Heart and Pink Floyd.

The list of names could go on and on and on.

As we come to the end of the Century, Britain and America continue to rule the world when it comes to Rock music.

The songs are listened to by young people on all continents but the bands are almost exclusively British or American.

The major exception was ABBA, whose performers came from Sweden and Norway. There are not many others.

Even the Bee Gees, based in Australia, were born and raised in Britain.

It is one of the most incredible tales of cultural domination in the Twentieth Century.

The monopoly can't go on forever, of course. But it will continue well into the new Century, creating employment for British musicians for many years to come.

Rock Groups: What You Said

Sarah Cooper and Sarah Taylor of Ashby-de-la-Zouch both voted for Aerosmith first, followed by Oasis and Bon Jovi.

Alan Gill of Leicester put Queen in first place.

"What more need I say about Queen: the impact they made over 20 years and the impact that Freddie Mercury's death made to the Aids awareness campaign."

He voted for Dire Straits second and Aerosmith third.

Ben Hancock of Glen Parva, Leicester, writes in praise of The Beatles: "I am only sixteen and yet I am obsessed with The Beatles. The Beatles were a phenomenon of the Sixties but their influence was felt in the Seventies and beyond. The Beatles were the greatest artists of all time.

"She Loves You, I Want To Hold Your Hand, I Feel Fine, Help!, Yesterday, In My Life, Hey Jude, Let it Be, The Long and Winding Road, are just some of the great songs that came from The Beatles and they are still the biggest selling artists to date.

"Other contenders would be the Doors and Beach Boys but, as I have already stressed, they don't come anywhere near The Beatles."

Mr. D. Sharman of Nuneaton writes: "Here is my list of all time Rock bands for the poll you are doing: first, Eagles; second, Fleetwood Mac; third, Dire Straits; fourth R.E.M.; fifth, Eurythmics."

Alan Bolt of Birstall: "I am writing to vote for The Kinks, who are quite clearly the greatest Rock 'N' Roll band of the Century.

"They invented Heavy Metal with songs such as You Really Got Me and All Day and All of the Night and Punk Rock with tracks like I

The Beatles, on a visit to the De Montfort Hall, Leicester in 1964.
(Photo from Leicester Mercury)

From the top: Yes;
Deep Purple – Jon Lord (front right), main composer for the group, is a Leicester man;
The Jam, punk rock pioneers, in 1978;
Pink Floyd in 1967: Rick Wright, Roger Waters, Nick Mason and Syd Barrett;
Angus Young of AC/DC;
Wet Wet Wet in 1988;
Dave and Ann of Eurythmics in 1981;
Sting from Police, in 1982.

Below right: ABBA, pictured after winning the Eurovision Song Contest at Brighton, in 1974, launching them to global stardom.

Need You and I'm Not Like Everybody Else."

David Fitzhugh of Leicester writes: "My vote for the top rock band of the century has to be The Jam because of songs like In the City, English Rose, News of the World, This is the Modern World.

"To me, these are classics; excellent new wave sounds. Second is Joy Division, with haunting vocals from the late Ian Curtis and depressing songs. They sum up a tragic but incredible band, performing in the late 1970s.

"Third is The Doors, not for Jim Morrison but the fantastic keyboard playing of Ray Manzarack, in the Sixties.

"Fourth is Electric Prunes, a late Sixties American psychedelic band. I Had Too Much to Dream Last Night is a classic track.

"Fifth is The Cure, active in the 1970s and 1980s."

Ashley Cropper, rock specialist for HMV, Leicester, writes to say his favourite rock band of the century is The Beach Boys, followed by Stone Roses, The Beatles and Manic Street Preachers.

He says there were thousands of new rock bands in the last ten to fifteen years and many of them are very good.

"A selection of the biggest and best would include: U2, The Verve, Stone Roses, Oasis, Radiohead, REM, Manic Street Preachers, Metallica, Nirvana, Dire Straits, Guns 'N' Roses and Smashing Pumpkins."

Jon Garland of Leicester, who had earlier voted on the Internet for The Jam, used the Internet again to send the following additional nominations: "Tubeway Army. They were one of the most innovative bands of the past 25 years. Their music was dark, brooding and ethereal and they set the tone for the techno era to come."

He also cast a vote for The Clash.

Jan Baxter of Oadby: "I would like to vote for Bon Jovi.

"At the latter part of the Eighties, Bon Jovi were undoubtedly the biggest Rock Band in the world.

"They sold out Wembley Stadium three nights running in 1996 on a tour promoting their album, These Days, which knocked Michael Jackson off number one.

"They are a group of highly articulate, intelligent, socially aware, but above all fun and music loving individuals who, when grouped together, are the ultimate Rock Band of the Century."

Rebecca Makin: "First, Queen; second, The Beatles; third, Aerosmith.

Top left: the Bee Gees in 1981
Top Right: Queen in 1991. (© Queen Productions, Photograph by Simon Fowler)

"What more do I have to say? Queen changed and expanded music, touching every style imaginable and influencing countless other musicians, as well as bringing pleasure to millions."

E. Quinn of Leicester: "My first choice of the very best rock band of the Century is without any doubt at all: The Beatles. They had such an unbelievably wide variety of original songs as well as their great performances.

"Second, ABBA, uncopyable and original.

"Third, the Bee Gees, but with reservations as I didn't care for the high-pitched material.

"Fourth, The Beach Boys, for their vitality.

"Fifth, Procul Harem, not many hits but well done."

Catherine Siroky-Holder of Ratby, Leics.: "First, Queen; second, Aerosmith; third, Guns 'N' Roses.

"Naturally it has to be Queen, doesn't it?

"Four extremely talented individuals, who together made up the best, most original and most influential rock group in the history of music. Who can even come close to Freddie's dynamic vocal expertise? Who plays guitar like Brian? Who writes such politically mind-provoking songs as Roger and who can reach the high notes in the way he can?

"Who is as quiet and yet as level-headed as John?

"And what song has ever been comparable to Bohemian Rhapsody?"

Bill Wood of Leicester Forest East: "Forget all your heavy metal and new wave rubbish! Give local talent some credit! Showaddywaddy made some good records and put Leicester on the map.

"They're a fine Leicester band and I'm proud of them. For me, they are number one!"

His selections: "First, Showaddywaddy; second, The Beatles; third, Rubettes; fourth, Glitter Band; fifth, ABBA."

Mary Hickinbotham: "I think The Beatles were the best group of the Century and the Bee Gees were next. Then came the Rolling Stones and fourth comes Showaddywaddy and fifth is Jimi Hendrix."

Left: Showaddywaddy at the stage door of Leicester's De Montfort Hall in 1974.
Back row: Dave, Trev, Malcolm and Rod; Front row: Geoff, Romeo, Buddy and Russ. (Photo from Leicester Mercury)

Chapter Seven
Champions of Your Century : 1900 – 1999
MUSICALS AND DISNEY ANIMATED FILMS

When people begin to list their choices for the greatest cinema films of the Century, they usually end up by saying: "Of course I forgot to mention all those great musicals and Disney animated films."

Well, we didn't forget.

In fact before beginning the search for the best films of all time, we will start by listing some of the top candidates from among the century's outstanding musicals and Disney productions.

The musicals produced many happy memories. Titles leap readily to mind.

And so do the performers. Gene Kelly, Cliff Richard, Elvis Presley, Fred Astaire (with Ginger Rogers), John Travolta (with Olivia Newton John), Judy Garland, Bing Crosby, Frank Sinatra and, of course, Julie Andrews.

The nomination lists have been debated for years. The films at or near the top always seem to include The Sound of Music, Mary Poppins, My Fair Lady, Singing in the Rain, West Side Story, An American in Paris and Gigi.

The major British titles include the Beatles in Hard Days Night and Help; Cliff Richard in The Young Ones and Summer Holiday; the Dickens classic, Oliver!, and the only two Andrew Lloyd Webber musicals to make it into the cinema, Jesus Christ Superstar and Evita.

Looking at this list it's obvious Hollywood owes Britain a debt of gratitude for producing so many story ideas as well as stars.

From top:
West Side Story (1961, United Artists, directed by Jerome Robbins and Robert Wise).
***Singin' in the Rain*, starring and co-directed by Gene Kelly** (1952, MGM, Stanley Donan and Gene Kelly) (photo courtesy Camera Press).
***My Fair Lady* - Rex Harrison and Audrey Hepburn** (1964, 20th Century Fox, directed by George Cukor).

Left: Frank Sinatra and Bing Crosby in *High Society*. (1956, Paramount Pictures, directed by Charles Walters.)
Right: *Fiddler on the Roof*. (1971, Mirisch Company, directed by Norman Jewison.)

Having said that, there is no doubt America was the centre of the cinema musical for most of this Century.

The great titles go on and on. The Wizard of Oz, Yankee Doodle Dandy, Grease, the Mickey Rooney-Judy Garland hit Babes on Broadway, the Gene Kelly-Frank Sinatra-Kathryn Grayson hit Anchors Aweigh, The Glenn Miller Story, the Betty Grable-John Payne-Carmen Miranda-Harry James success Springtime in the Rockies, the Barbra Streisand hit Funny Girl and Frank Sinatra and Marlon Brando in Guys and Dolls.

Besides The Sound of Music, the best Rodgers and Hammerstein productions are: Oklahoma, Carousel (featuring You'll Never Walk Alone), South Pacific and The King and I.

In the very beginning, Al Jolson launched the era of talking pictures in 1927 with the first musical film, The Jazz Singer, and his voice was featured in the 1946 musical biography, The Jolson Story.

If you're over 39 you may also remember Flying Down to Rio and the great Nelson Eddy-Jeanette MacDonald hits, Maytime, Naughty Marietta and New Moon.

Later Bing Crosby played opposite Frank Sinatra in High Society (featuring the classic duet of the Cole Porter number, What a Swell Party This Is). Crosby also joined Danny Kaye in the seasonal classic, White Christmas.

The Elvis Presley musicals always had great singing but a limp plot. The best of the Elvis musicals is probably Blue Hawaii, a magical combination of wonderful songs and a watchable story, ending with two on a raft on their way to be married. In this case, Elvis, the groom, was more gorgeous than the bride. Well, he was the star, after all.

The wedding scene begins with the perfect four words. The raft begins its journey across the lake. Elvis and his girl are hand-in-hand. The wedding ceremony is about to begin. There is music in the air. Elvis begins to sing: "This is the moment."

It has been called the most romantic wedding in the history of the cinema.

If a musical is judged by the songs alone, perhaps West Side Story should be at or near the top.

When it first opened, there was an intermission at half time.

A popcorn salesman told me the following anecdote.

The first person to emerge into the lobby was a man about twenty-five who was humming and then burst loudly into song, "Tonight, tonight…" He suddenly realised he wasn't alone and he trailed off, embarrassed.

A few seconds later a man and women emerged, both singing, "There's only you tonight…." Everybody laughed. It was a wonderful moment and a tribute to a landmark film.

However, the depressing story, a remake of Romeo and Juliet, prevented many people from going back to see it again, unlike some of the happier films.

It's difficult to imagine The Wizard of Oz without Judy Garland. In fact, the script was written for 11-year-old Shirley Temple. When she wasn't available, the studio scurried around and decided to try to salvage the picture by using 17-year-old Judy Garland, dressed in a blonde wig and with doll face make-up.

After several screen tests, they abandoned the Shirley Temple look and let Judy be herself. The rest, as they say, is history. She made the film a success and it launched her acting and singing career. Over the Rainbow became one of the top hits of the first forty years of the Century.

Meanwhile, we also began the search for the greatest Disney animated films.

For convenience, they are divided into two groups. A. Those supervised by Walt Disney during his lifetime and B. The later films produced by the Disney Corporation, carrying on his work.

Category A: Snow White and the Seven Dwarfs, Pinocchio, Fantasia, Dumbo, Bambi, Cinderella, Alice in Wonderland, Peter Pan, Lady and the Tramp, Sleeping Beauty, The Sword in the Stone and 101 Dalmatians.

Category B: Winnie the Pooh, The Lion King, Beauty and the Beast, The Jungle

Above: *Lady and the Tramp* **(1955);**
From top right: *One-hundred-and-one Dalmations* **(1961);** *Dumbo* **(1941);** *Bambi* **(1942)**
(All pictures on this page © Walt Disney Productions.)

Book, The Aristocats, Robin Hood, The Rescuers, Aladdin, Pocahontas, The Fox and the Hound, The Little Mermaid, Hercules, and the Hunchback of Notre Dame.

We hope, at last, to find out if Bambi was better than Snow White and the Seven Dwarfs and whether either of them was as good as The Lion King or Beauty and the Beast.

The debate has been going on for up to fifty years. One of the advantages of being around near the end of a century is that all these questions will, at last, be answered.

Above left: *Fantasia* **(1940);**
centre right: *Peter Pan* **(1953);**
bottom: *Cinderella* **(1950).**

From top right: *Aristocats* **(1970);** *The Little Mermaid* **(1989);** *Pocahontas* **(1995);** *Pinocchio* **(1940);** *The Sword in the Stone* **(1963);** *The Hunchback of Notre Dame* **(1996);** *The Many Adventures of Winnie the Pooh* **(1977);** *Aladdin* **(1992).**

(All pictures on this page © Walt Disney Productions.)

Chapter Eight
Champions of Your Century : 1900 – 1999
CINEMA FILMS

Dear Meryl Streep: I was reading in the newspaper how angry you are about the way the American Film Institute carried out the voting for the top cinema films of the century. You said the (male) organisers waited until most of the females were out of the hall at committee meetings before the ballots were distributed and therefore the election was not a fair result.

Well, Meryl, all I know about it is what I've read in the newspapers but I can assure you everyone has had an equal chance to vote here in Leicestershire and Rutland as we launched the search for the Outstanding Cinema Film of the Century.

We invited everyone to send letters listing their top choices for the top ten films of all time.

Since 1950, panels of experts have been busy making lists of the best films. The consensus in mid-century was that the top three were: 1. Gone With the Wind 2. Casablanca and 3. Citizen Kane.

The process was such fun they continued to revise their selections year after year and by 1960 a clear trend had developed. The Orson Welles film began to sink out of sight while Casablanca and Gone With the Wind took turns being numbers one and two.

Maybe, I have no way of knowing, the exclusion of female

From top:
***Four Weddings and a Funeral,* starring Kristin Scott Thomas and Hugh Grant.** (1994, Polygram, directed by Mike Newell.)
Star Wars. (1977, Star Wars Productions, directed by George Lucas.)
***Gone With The Wind.* Clark Gable and Leslie Howard are seen here in Margaret Mitchell's US civil war epic.** (1939, Selznick International Pictures, directed by Victor Fleming.)

Right: *Citizen Kane.* (1941, RKO Radio Pictures, Starring and Directed by Orson Welles.);

Below: Gandhi – Richard Attenborough's epic film, starring Ben Kingsley. (1982, Columbia Pictures, directed by Richard Attenborough)

voters in the American Film Institute's new list could explain the surprising re-emergence of Citizen Kane into first place (from about 25th in a previous survey). The top five choices in the AFI voting: 1. Citizen Kane, 2. Casablanca, 3. The Godfather, 4. Gone With the Wind, 5. Lawrence of Arabia.

In any case, we started from the beginning in our search for the Outstanding Cinema Film of the Century. Everyone had an equal chance to vote.

When looking for serious contenders for the title, one place to begin was the Oscar winners for Best Film of the Year.

On this basis there was Titanic, Ben Hur, Rocky, The English Patient, Forrest Gump, Amadeus, Gandhi, Chariots of Fire, Kramer vs. Kramer,

Charlton Heston in *Ben Hur*. (1959, MGM, directed by William Wyler.);

Annie Hall, Patton, Tom Jones, The Bridge on the River Kwai, On the Waterfront, Mrs. Miniver and It Happened One Night.

Of course there are all those fabulous musicals, including the Oscar winners for Best picture: The Sound of Music, Gigi, My Fair Lady, Oliver! and West Side Story, along with the great Disney films.

There are zillions more candidates to consider, including The Wizard of Oz, E.T., Star Wars, It's a Wonderful Life, Some Like It Hot, Doctor Zhivago, Jaws, Raiders of the Lost Ark, Elmer Gantry, Brief Encounter, Who's Afraid of Virginia Woolf? and Alien.

Also Four Weddings and a Funeral, Shirley Valentine, Working Girl, Ghost, Sense and Sensibility (and all the other great Jane Austen films), along with Roger Rabbit, Space Jam, National Velvet and Lassie Come Home.

The list could go on forever.

Letters came in listing hundreds of possible candidates but it eventually became clear the spotlight would turn on ten films as the major candidates.

One was Gone With the Wind which was made in 1939, a mere twelve years after the very first talking picture. It is bewildering to comprehend how film-making could have improved so much, so quickly, and also why it does not seem to have progressed very far since 1939. Why is a film so ancient still one of the top contenders for the title of the best ever? There is no question it continues to be regarded as one of the greatest films of all time.

Some new ideas were introduced by Orson Welles in 1941 with Citizen Kane but, while it was greatly admired, it was criticised at the time for being a film that's difficult to love.

Along came Casablanca in 1942, the right film at the right time, a happy accident. It was just one of hundreds being churned out that year and nobody expected much of it.

But the war was on. When Ingrid Bergman told Humphrey Bogart: "I love you so much and I hate this war so much," she seemed to be speaking for every woman concerned about the fate of civilisation and the man she loved.

There are seven worthy challengers to these three classic films.

For example, there are three great epic films from the post-war years.

Two were by David Lean. Lawrence of Arabia is regarded by critics as his best work while Dr. Zhivago was one of the great romantic films of the Century and its reputation was greatly helped by the haunting Lara's Theme.

During the past twenty years there has been a tendency for reviewers to divide everything into action pictures or women's films.

Looking back at the work of David Lean, the critics label Lawrence as a man's film and Zhivago a woman's romance.

If you announce this view at a social gathering you'll find a great horde of women stepping forward to say how much they loved Lawrence of Arabia and an equal number of men singing the praises of Dr. Zhivago. Clearly, trying to pin labels on films is a dicey business.

The third great epic of the post-war era is Ben Hur, one of the most-honoured films of the Century.

It was a personal triumph for Charlton Heston and, despite its great length, was entertaining from start to finish. Incredibly, Heston was so impressed by the script he signed to do the picture without knowing what role he would be playing.

It was eventually decided he would be the hero while young and handsome Stephen Boyd would be the villain. Either way, Heston just wanted to be part of it. It was a good decision. The film won eleven Academy Awards, including one for Charlton Heston as best actor.

That leaves the four challengers from the modern era. The two from Britain are Shakespeare In Love and Four Weddings and a Funeral.

The Shakespeare film was a tribute to Britain's literary man of the Millennium. It was cleverly written so that Shakespeare and the woman he admires become Romeo and Juliet on stage near the final curtain. The climax all comes together neatly, thanks to Judi Dench in a brief appearance as the great Queen Elizabeth.

Meanwhile, Four Weddings and a Funeral was seen as a breath of fresh air, innovative and amusing, and made a deserved impact in all of the English-speaking world. Its lasting reputation would seem to depend upon how its star, Hugh Grant, is viewed, say, in 2020, two decades from now.

This leaves two epics from America as the remaining challengers for the title.

Titanic was the sensation of 1997, greatly helped by the theme song by Celine Dion, My Heart Will Go On. The movie was highly praised and dominated the Academy Awards presentations for its year.

Again, following a new trend in film criticism, Titanic was labelled the greatest woman's film of the Century. When this was announced there were many protests from men who said they also felt it was a great film and the label was unfair.

Titanic, **starring Leonardo DiCaprio and Kate Winslet.** (1997, 20th Century Fox, directed by James Cameron.)

The critics responded by referring to an exit poll from a Titanic preview performance. Of all those who said they enjoyed the film "very much", 64 per cent were female.

In any event, we come now to the final challenger, Star Wars.

When the film won its place among the Top Ten films there were only three Star Wars films, from earlier in the Century. Since that time, of course, there is a new Star Wars film and we are surrounded by the mega-hype associated with the release of a very expensive motion picture. Some people see this as brilliant timing for their favourite film while others viewed it as unfair in terms of its impact on the election for the greatest film of all time.

Films and Musicals: What You Said

The family of Mr. B. Lord of Birstall send the following votes.

"Our choices for the top ten films of the Century are (in order): Gone With the Wind, Random Harvest, Mrs. Miniver, Bonnie and Clyde, Casablanca, Stagecoach, Zulu, The Quiet Man, Rear Window and The Greatest Show on Earth.

"Our choices for the top ten musical films are (in order): The Sound of Music, Seven Brides for Seven Brothers, The Jolson Story, State Fair (the Jeanne Crain, Dana Andrews version), Spring Parade, (with Deanna Durban), Anchors Aweigh, Singin' in the Rain, You Were Never Lovelier (Astaire and Hayworth), Easter Parade and This is the Army."

Mrs. B.A. Hames of Leicester writes: "My vote for best musical is The Sound of Music."

In the category of Best Cinema Film of the Century, Mrs. V.A. Joyce of Birstall writes: "My nominations are (in order): Gone With the Wind, The King and I, Inn of the Sixth Happiness, My Fair Lady and The Greatest Story Every Told, the life of Jesus."

In addition, we welcomed two ballots by way of the Internet.

W.A. Kettel of Syston sends, by way of e-mail, the following votes:

"My choices (in order) for the top Musicals are: Grease, The Wizard of Oz and The Sound of Music."

Also by way of the Internet: Steve Norris of Long Whatton, votes for the following titles in the category of Best Film of the Century. His choices (in order) are:

"The Sting, Jurassic Park, The Shawshank Redemption.

"Despite what people say about the story content of Jurassic Park, I don't believe any film has ever delivered a total cinema experience through tension, thrills, sound and state of the art visual effects that this film has accomplished."

"The outstanding film of the Century surely has to be Gone With the Wind," writes Alan Edwards.

"Its essential appeal is that of a romantic story with strong characters and an impeccable production. The part of Rhett Butler seems to have been written for Clark Gable and, after a long search, Vivien Leigh was selected to play Scarlett. It was a superb performance that brought rave reviews and enhanced her career.

"Who could forget the burning of Atlanta? I never tire of listening to the musical score. It all brings back an era of tranquillity and romance of the 1930s."

Other films he feels should also be considered: Yankee Doodle Dandy ("James Cagney goes back to his roots as a hoofer and won a well-deserved Oscar, but wouldn't it all have been enhanced if it was in colour?"), Easter Parade, Singing in the Rain, Casablanca, a number of Errol Flynn films such as Adventures of Robin Hood, Charge of the Light Brigade and The Sea Hawk plus other Humphrey Bogart films such as African Queen and Maltese Falcon.

The top three films selected by Barry Goodacre of Loughborough are: 1. Gone With the Wind, 2. Casablanca and 3. Love is a Many-Splendored Thing.

His other choices include Psycho, Random Harvest, Twelve Angry Men and The Old Dark Horse.

Ian Holdridge of Fleckney votes for: "Citizen Kane, absolutely flawless, High Noon, a classic western, Chariots of Fire, the best of British, Gone With the Wind, unforgettable, The Godfather, riveting, In the Heat of the Night, tension packed with superb performances by Sidney Poitier and Rod Steiger, and Invasion of the Body Snatchers, forget the daft title, it's a sci-fi masterpiece."

Colin Fraser of Market Harborough writes: "My vote for film of the Century goes to E.T. Others I like include Lawrence of Arabia, Out of Africa, Gone With the Wind, The Big Country, Ben Hur and The Magnificent Seven."

William H. Brooks of Leicester votes for (in no particular order): Lawrence of Arabia, Fantasia, War and Peace, Birth of a Nation, The General.

Joan Brooks selects (in order): 1. Ryan's Daughter, 2. It's a Wonderful Life, 3. Dr. Zhivago, 4. Citizen Kane and 5. The Deerhunter.

The five selections by Bob Norton of Leicester are: Valley of the Giants, High Noon, High Sierra, Mr. Hulot's Holiday and the Humphrey Bogart film, Dead End.

Nearing the finish line, the top candidates for best musical film were:

The Sound of Music, Grease, Wizard of Oz, My Fair Lady, Mary Poppins, Oliver!, Singin' in the Rain, A Hard Days Night,

Grease, starring John Travolta and Olivia Newton John. (1978, Paramount Pictures, directed by Rendal Kleiser.)

Above left: Judy Garland in *The Wizard of Oz.* (1939, MGM, directed by Victor Fleming.)
Above right: *Mary Poppins*, starring Julie Andrews. (1964, Walt Disney Productions, directed by Robert Stevenson.)
Below left: *Forrest Gump*, starring Tom Hanks. (1994, Paramount Pictures, directed by Robert Zemeckis)**;**
Below centre: Yul Brynner, Ingrid Bergman and Helen Hayes in *Anastasia* (1976, 20th Century Fox)**.**
Below right: *The English Patient*, starring Ralph Fiennes and Kristin Scott Thomas. (1996, Miramax/Tiger Moth Productions, directed by Anthony Minghuella.)**;**

The King and I, South Pacific.

White Christmas, Seven Brides for Seven Brothers, The Glenn Miller Story, Calamity Jane, Maytime, West Side Story, Naughty Marietta, Oklahoma, High Society, An American in Paris, Gigi, Anchors Aweigh, Love Me or Leave Me and Evita.

Meanwhile, many readers said it was difficult to choose only three or four candidates from so many films.

We were delighted by the solution sent in by Mr. P. Webb of Birstall, Leicester.

First he worked out the best from each decade and that helped him to narrow down the contenders to a manageable level. Once you narrow the list, the rest is easy.

He wrote: "Regarding the greatest films of the Century. Each decade has produced many that could be considered. Here are my choices.

"The 1930s: Gone With the Wind, North West Passage, Wizard of Oz.

"The 1940s: Magnificent Ambersons, Meet Me in St. Louis, Double Indemnity.

"The 1950s: Ben Hur, Singin' in the Rain, The Searchers.

"The 1960s: Butch Cassidy and the Sundance Kid, Psycho, The Graduate.

"The 1970s: Picnic at Hanging Rock, Don't Look Now, Close Encounters of the Third Kind.

"The 1980s: Witness, Fanny and Alexander, E.T.

"The 1990s: Titanic, Dances with Wolves, Saving Private Ryan.

"And the winners are: In third place, Psycho, in second place, Butch Cassidy and the Sundance Kid and the winner is: BEN HUR.

Similarly, his verdict on the greatest musicals of the Century: "In third place, Wizard of Oz, in second place, Meet Me in St. Louis and the winner is: SINGING IN THE RAIN."

His choices may be open to debate but the process is brilliant. When faced with so many good candidates, narrow them down decade by decade until there are only a handful of contenders to consider. That makes the final decision easy – and fun.

Here are the final choices from other voters.

Margaret Ford of Wigston: "For me, the best film of all time is Dr. Zhivago. I have watched it many, many times. Close behind are The Third Man and Casablanca.

"The greatest musical ever has to be The Sound of Music. I have the video and I have watched it more times than I can count. The recent musical of Evita, featuring Madonna, also comes high up on my list.

"My husband's favourite is Carousel."

Colin Fraser of Market Harborough: "My top three musical films are: West Side Story, The Sound of Music and The King and I."

Laura Rosewarne of Leicester: "Here are my choices for the top films of all time:

"1. Gone With the Wind: I am a huge Vivien Leigh fan. This film has everything.

"2. Grease: No matter how many times you see this, the tunes are always great to listen to."

She also liked The Highlander, Star Wars and Big.

Richard Javor of Newbold Verdon votes for: War and Peace, The Adventures of Robin Hood, Gone With the Wind, Dr. Zhivago and the Johnny Weissmuller version of Tarzan of the Apes.

Above: Danny Kaye and Bing Crosby in *White Christmas* (1954, Paramount Pictures, directed by Michael Curtiz);
Below: *The King and I*, featuring Yul Brynner and Deborah Kerr (1956, 20th Century Fox, directed by Walter Lang).

Julie Andrews with the von Trapp family in *The Sound of Music*. (1965, 20th Century Fox, directed by Robert Wise.)

His choices in the category of top musical film: Maytime, Rose Marie, Naughty Marietta, My Fair Lady, Oliver!, Mary Poppins, The Sound of Music, Wizard of Oz, Singin' in the Rain and The King and I.

Jeff Alden of Market Harborough: "I should like to vote for A Room with a View as my film of the century.

"It is, in my opinion, a masterpiece with amazing performances from Maggie Smith, Daniel Day-Lewis and Denholm Elliot, among others.

"My other nominations are: A Man for all Seasons, Godfather 2, the Kenneth Brannagh version of Henry V, The 1960 version of The Time Machine and The Shooting Party."

From John Coles of Wigston: "Here are my choices for the best cinema film of the Century. 1. Casablanca (for the stars, story and pure Hollywood authenticity of the production) 2. Dr. Zhivago (for the cinematic sweep, photography, story and music; a lasting tribute to David Lean) and 3. High Noon (Gary Cooper's portrayal of the law man's integrity and growing unease unfolded in a convincing way and could not be bettered.)"

His top choice for the musical film of the century is: The Sound of Music ("This supreme example of film-making stands out because of the setting, story, acting, colour and, above all, the music and singing to make this a memorable film.")

From Dan and Barbara Harding of Leicester: "Our choices for the Best Films of the Century are: 1. Gone With the Wind, 2. Dr. Zhivago, 3. Star Wars, 4. Ben Hur and 5. The Big Country.

"Our choices for the best musicals are: 1. The Sound of Music, 2. My Fair Lady, 3. The King and I, 4. Mary Poppins and 5. Paint Your Wagon."

From Dorothy H. Davis: "The outstanding film of the century is undoubtedly Ben Hur. I remember as a girl seeing the original version with Ramon Novarro as Ben Hur. I have never forgotten it and longed to see it again – and Charlton Heston as Ben Hur is magnificent.

"I am in my 90th year and have never seen another film to equal it."

Her choice for the greatest musical of the century is The Sound of Music.

From Faith Williams of Oadby: "I was surprised not to see to date a vote for On The Waterfront from your readers as the best cinema film of the century. This masterpiece from the 1950s is Marlon Brando's greatest performance and is THE performance of the century in the cinema.

"There is a powerful message in this film. One person can make a difference by standing up to bullying in all its forms.

"My vote for the best Musical goes to Guys and Dolls, a slick, witty, tuneful musical with (again) Marlon Brando and 'the voice of the century', Frank Sinatra."

Michel Hooper-Immins of Western Park, Leicester: "Casablanca has to be the classic film of all time. I know all the words – it is a timeless story and I could watch it forever.

"My other favourites are Calamity Jane (I don't like cowboy films but what a wonderful musical experience), The Wizard of Oz (I cried over this film as a child and it again has a timeless and everlasting appeal), Meet Me in St. Louis (Judy Garland at her best in another musical blockbuster), The Glenn Miller Story (A chance to hear some favourite tunes) and Summer Holiday (The Shadows playing among the hayricks of Yugoslavia)"

Roy Harper of Leicester: "My selections are 1. Gone With the Wind, 2. Casablanca and 3. Love Me or Leave Me (This mainly because of Doris Day who in my opinion is the best female singer ever)."

Mrs. L. J. Adams of Ratby, Leicester: "A memorable film of the Century has to be one that you can watch again and again and still be amazed and surprised by the quality of the script and the performance of the actors.

"There are so many classic films to choose from, but here are my selections: 1. Rebecca, 2. It Happened One Night, 3. Gone With the Wind, 4. The Quiet Man, 5. Singin' in the Rain."

Eunice Hamilton of Leicester: "My choices for outstanding film of the century are 1. Amadeus, 2. The Deerhunter, 3. Brief Encounter, 4. All This and Heaven Too, 5. Camelot.

"I have also enclosed the choices of my daughter. They are: 1. The African Queen, 2. Lawrence of Arabia, 3. The Madness of King George, 4. Shirley Valentine and 5. The Prime of Miss Jean Brodie."

Four members of the Johnson family of Braunstone sent in the follow selections.

Mrs. Cheryl Johnson (top five, in order): "Gone With the Wind, The King and I, Clash of the Titans, Stardust and Scream."

Mr. Andrew Johnson: "Aliens 2, Predator, Apollo 13, Battle of Britain, Enemy Mine."

Adam Johnson, age 10: "Jurassic Park, Jurassic Park 2, Jumanji, Batman, James and the Giant Peach."

Marie Johnson, age 9: "Cinderella, Babe, James and the Giant Peach, Snow White and the Seven Dwarfs and Jumanji."

Dennis J. Duggan of Leicester: "My favourite film is Spartacus, starring Kirk Douglas. The slave army are promised leniency if they will identify Spartacus. Kirk Douglas stands up and says 'I am Spartacus'. Man after man stands up and says the same. Who can fail to be moved by such a scene?"

His other selections, in order, are: Ben Hur, Bullitt, Brief Encounter and Airplane, the Leslie Nielson comedy.

The choices of his wife, Stephanie Duggan, are: "Airplane, Bambi, Dr. Zhivago, Fantasia and Omen 3."

Above: *The Jungle Book* (1967).
Below: *Snow White*, Disney's first full length film. (1937).
(Both pictures © Walt Disney Productions.)

Chapter Nine
Champions of Your Century : 1900 – 1999
VOICES

The 20th Century was a time of great oratory. Some voices dominated the scene and will linger with us well beyond the year 2000. These people include Winston Churchill, Richard Burton, The Queen, Mahatma Gandhi, FDR, John F. Kennedy and the civil rights leader Martin Luther King Jr.

All of these people will have an abiding place in history as long as the spoken word is available on record, in film or on video.

The list is not large, until you begin to consider the voices of popular entertainers – and then the names come rolling out by the hundreds.

The challenge then becomes to sift down the candidates to find the top ten voices of the Century. There were several obvious candidates.

Winston Churchill's speeches inspired Britain to hold on and fight, despite the odds, and never surrender.

Richard Burton's voice and his powerhouse talent made him famous around the world.

FDR assured Americans they would survive the horrors of the Depression, declaring "We have nothing to fear but fear itself."

The Queen has been an inspiration to the world for more than half a century, starting with her famous radio broadcasts to America as a child, "My Sister and I....."

The oratory of Mahatma Gandhi changed the lives of millions of people in India.

The voice of John F. Kennedy was an inspiration to the free world and was a driving force for change, especially for the young.

The American disciple of Gandhi, Martin Luther King Jr., changed his nation when he declared that he had a dream that some day his children would be judged by the nature of their character and not the colour of their skin in his famous speech, I Have A Dream Today.

In Britain, other prominent candidates include Prime Minister Lloyd George, actors Laurence Olivier, Glenda Jackson, Ralph Richardson and John Gielgud, along with the great poet, Dylan Thomas.

In the 20th Century, according to taste, the voice of France could be either Charles DeGaulle or Maurice Chevalier.

In 1917 Lenin took control of Russia by the power of his oratory and the force of arms, changing the country into a Communist state, and in Germany there were many strident voices that led to the two great wars.

At the same time there was in America the quiet rhythmic voice of a teen-aged evangelist, Billy Graham, who became the religious adviser to that nation for more than 50 years.

But, back to the entertainers.

When it comes to voice, the first actor on everyone's list is Richard Burton.

It was generally agreed he had a wonderful talent that was largely

Top: Gandhi outside No 10 Downing Street.
Middle: Queen Elizabeth II in 1973.
Bottom: Winston Churchill and Franklin D. Roosevelt at the Yalta Conference in 1945.

Far left: Lawrence Olivier in 1954, as *Richard III* (1956, London Film Productions/ Carlton International Media Ltd.)
left: Richard Burton as O'Brian in the film of George Orwell's *1984*. (1984, Virgin Films./20th Century Fox)
Below left: John Wayne, in *Wake of the Red Witch* (1949, Republic Pictures Corp.)
Below right: Katharine Hepburn in *Desk Set* (1957, 20th Century Fox).

wasted but on occasion showed through magnificently.

According to the famous director Mike Nichols, Burton was at his awesome best in the 12-minute soliloquy in Who's Afraid of Virginia Woolf ? when out in the garden he begins: "When I was sixteen and going to prep school."

Nichols said he couldn't believe what happened next. Burton went through the entire soliloquy without a pause. In one take it was absolutely perfect.

Nichols said: "I've never seen anything like it. That achievement alone should have won him the Academy Award."

He was nominated but of course he didn't win. His wild behaviour, including singing Welsh ballads at Hollywood parties at the top of his voice at 3 a.m., cost him many votes. Many women thought he was wonderful and that was another problem.

But the greatest test of his fabulous voice was yet to come.

One night at a party Burton met Robert Kennedy, the president's brother. Kennedy bet that he could recite the alphabet backwards perfectly. Having practised the trick he won the bet. Burton, in trying to match the feat, made a buffoon of himself.

However, he countered by doubling the bet and saying he could decline the verb "to be" and do it so well it would win an ovation on national television.

I happened to be watching television the night Burton appeared on a talk show. He asked permission to recite a little poem.

To a large television audience he emoted: "I am. (Pause for dramatic effect) You….are. (He raises an octave and pauses again.) He is. (quietly and slowly- again a pause.) We….are. (Triumpantly) You…are. (Rising in inflection to the climax) (Long pause – shouting) THEY are!" He got a thunderous ovation and won a large sum of money from Robert Kennedy. There was no denying the power of his voice.

Burton also came up against Winston Churchill in the battle of great voices.

A young Burton was playing Hamlet on stage when he heard a rumbling in the audience off to the left. It turned out to be Sir Winston, who was mumbling the lines aloud from memory. Burton said it sounded like an echo.

At intermission, Churchill came backstage and had a friendly chat with Hamlet and then announced he had to depart for a meeting. Burton thanked him for coming and heaved a sigh of relief that he was going. He didn't need competition of that calibre.

Laurence Olivier is one of the few actors who could match them both. Olivier's driving force was his passion to take chances. He would attempt things on the stage that no one else would dare, knowing the power of his voice, and his talent, would see him through.

Among the actresses, the voice of Glenda Jackson reigns supreme. She was absolutely superb playing the great Queen Elizabeth and won many awards.

There are other great entertainers whose voices will be remembered for many years. They include Cary Grant, Orson Welles, Bob Hope, Vivien Leigh, Katharine Hepburn, Ronald Colman, Anthony Hopkins, Gracie Fields and John Wayne.

Glenda Jackson as Elizabeth R. (1971, photo courtesy BBC)

There are hundreds more.

Sifting the list down to the top ten finalists was a difficult chore. This was one of the most competitive categories of all.

Voices: What You Said

From David Fitzhugh, Leicester: "My vote for Voice of the Century has to be Martin Luther King Jr. He was a great spokesman for his people, a speaker for all under-privileged people everywhere. He is still sadly missed by everyone who cares about injustice.

"Second, Winston Churchill. His words still say it all. We should be thankful to the few who did so much for so many – a great speech from a great man.

"Third, John F. Kennedy, a great spokesman and thinker for the free world.

"Princess Diana would have become one of the great speakers of our time if not for her untimely death."

Right from the beginning, letters in this category stated a name or two and then added the words, "and, of course, Winston Churchill."

The Queen was highly regarded for her talks on television and radio for more than fifty years.

Richard Burton, in his prime had a voice that could, it was said, melt any woman's heart.

The three American leaders also have a large following, especially Franklin Delano Roosevelt from the war years and Martin Luther King Jr. who was a respected and exciting voice working for racial tolerance and understanding.

Left: US President J. F. Kennedy on a visit to London in 1961.
Right: Dr Martin Luther King. (Photo by Karsh of Ottawa. Camera Press.)

Chapter Ten
Champions of Your Century : 1900 – 1999
POP SINGERS

Our search for the greatest pop singers of the Century began in May, 1998, at the Leicester Mercury's Transport Pageant at Abbey Park.

A total of 1,348 people came to our election booth to nominate their favourite performers.

It was a very happy afternoon.

Two women of uncertain age were all smiles. One of them said, "I'm always delighted to have the chance to vote for Elvis Presley. I hope he wins."

Her friend gave her a good-natured push. "Don't you dare! I want Cliff Richard to win."

There was more pushing, shoving and laughing as they put their ballots in the box. They confided they had reached a happy compromise. Elvis and Cliff were first and second on one ballot and second and first on the other.

A few minutes later, three lads, about ten years old, came to the booth.

One of them announced: "I want to vote for the Spice Girls."

Hearing that the vote was for individual singers, not groups, he replied: "But I'm in love with all of them."

From top: Freddie Mercury (Queen Productions Limited, photo by Neal Preston); **Elton John at the Empire Theatre, Liverpool, in 1976; Tom Jones; Phil Collins in concert with Genesis in 1980** (photo from Leicester Mercury); **Michael Jackson in 1987.** (Photo courtesy of EMI).

He and his friends held a meeting and tried to decide which of the girls to vote for. Eventually they got it sorted out, voted, and walked away singing a Spice Girls song.

A young married couple approached the voting booth eagerly. But then they started to quarrel.

He: "What do you mean, Elvis? Sinatra is a much better singer."

She: "But Elvis is better looking."

He: "It's about who is the best singer, not the best looking."

She: "I'd also like to vote for Engelbert. He's a very good singer. But I can't."

He: "Why not?"

She: "I can never remember how to spell his last name."

They both laughed. Leaving the booth, they compared notes. After their top choices they had both, by coincidence, voted for Elton John second.

They agreed it was easy to spell!

A woman helped her elderly mother to the booth.

"Mum wants to vote for Howard Keel," she announced. Then she whispered, "Don't tell her, but I'm going to vote for Tom Jones."

It was a wonderful way to spend a sunny afternoon.

The four male singers favoured on that afternoon were: Elton John, Elvis Presley, Frank Sinatra and Cliff Richard.

The favourite female singers were: Celine Dion who was a sensation thanks to the continuing

Left, from top: Bing Crosby (photo from *Holiday Inn*, 1942, Paramount); **Sammy Davis Junior; Mick Jagger singing with the Rolling Stones at Granby Halls, Leicester in 1976** (Photo from Leicester Mercury); **Engelbert Humperdinck in 1987.** (Photo from Leicester Mercury)

Above centre: Julie Andrews sings of her favourite things in *The Sound of Music* (1965, 20th Century Fox).
Above right: Judy Garland keeps up with Fred Astaire.
Right: John Lennon in 1964 on a visit to Leicester. (Photo from Leicester Mercury)

Clockwise from top: Whitney Houston in 1990 (photo courtesy BMG/Arista); **Vera Lynn** (photo courtesy BBC); **Madonna on Wogan in 1991** (photo courtesy BBC). **Celine Dion on the National Lottery Draw** (BBC, photo by Chris Capstick); **Tina Turner in 1984** (Photo courtesy EMI Parlaphone).

popularity of My Heart Will Go On, the top song from the film Titanic, and Madonna, who has been a major performer for many years.

Shirley Bassey also did well, along with Whitney Houston and Barbra Streisand.

In addition, there were stacks of other names put in nomination.

For the male singers they included:

Michael Jackson, Bryan Adams, Mick Jagger, John Lennon, Paul McCartney, Bing Crosby, Nat King Cole, Phil Collins and Mario Lanza.

Every handful of ballots brought new names to consider. Buddy Holly, Al Jolson, Bob Dylan, Perry Como, Louis Armstrong and Freddie Mercury.

The flood of votes for Celine Dion and Madonna made it clear from the first day that they would be among the top contenders for female pop singer of the Century.

It remained to be seen who their main challengers would be.

From the war years there were Judy Garland, Gracie Fields, Vera Lynn, Dinah Shore, Ella Fitzgerald, Ethel Merman, Lena Horne and Doris Day.

In the post-war era there were hundreds of new female superstars, notably Julie Andrews and Barbra Streisand. All of them were suggested as candidates for the top ten of the Century.

Additional names included Diana Ross, Tina Turner, Sarah Brightman, Rosemary Clooney, Olivia Newton John, Liza Minnelli, Cleo Laine, Karen Carpenter and Elaine Paige.

International singers like Piaf and Marlene Dietrich also won support.

Lead singers from bands were also eligible as solo performers. These include Annie Lennox, Debbie Harry of Blondie, the two ladies from ABBA and, of course, each of the Spice Girls.

Alas, none of the Spice Girls made the list of finalists.

Those who made it were, in alphabetical order, Julie Andrews, Shirley Bassey, Karen Carpenter, Celine Dion, Judy Garland, Whitney Houston, Vera Lynn, Madonna, Barbra Streisand and Tina Turner.

For the men, the top ten finalists were: Bryan Adams, Michael Jackson, John Lennon, Elton John, Tom Jones, Paul McCartney, Freddie Mercury, Elvis Presley, Cliff Richard and Frank Sinatra.

Pop Singers: What You Said

Ed Keywood: "I would agree that the singers mentioned all had much to offer but Vera Lynn has to be the one!"

Mrs. J. Conway of Leicester: "My first choice is Shirley Bassey, with Dusty Springfield second. They are both excellent."

Sheila Vickers, Houghton on the Hill, Leics: "The top choice for me is Doris Day, then Shirley Bassey, but Judith Durham should be considered too."

Barbara J. Wood of Mountsorrel, Leics: "After a great deal of thought, my first vote goes to Liza Minnelli. I think she is better than her mother (and I liked Judy Garland) but Liza has a good range and has sung with many top male singers (the late, great Sinatra, Sammy Davis Jr. and the Pet Shop Boys). She's a very talented lady. My other considerations are Ella Fitzgerald and Shirley Bassey."

On the subject of male singers, Barbara writes: "To me there can be only one winner, Ol' Blue Eyes himself, Frank Sinatra. Elvis was and is very popular but not for me. My top choice is Frank Sinatra."

Michael Peter Wallis of Leics: "I choose Judy Garland. Barbra Streisand comes very close as a seller of a song; as does Shirley Bassey, probably the most emotive. I have no idea how Rosemary Clooney could be high on anybody's list; or Madonna."

Barry Goodacre of Loughborough, Leics: "My top choice is Dinah Shore, followed by Alice Faye, Julie London, Carole Carr and Rosemary Clooney. I regarded Gracie Fields more as a comedienne than a singer. During the war I thought Anne Shelton was a better singer than Vera Lynn but she didn't get such good songs."

John Challis of Melton Mowbray, Leics., is a Frank Sinatra fan.

"It really started for me back in the middle 1950s after I heard the recording of Songs For Swingin' Lovers. After that I went back to his early days and realised what I had missed in my youth. Frank Sinatra was streets ahead of the rest in all departments. It was the grounding with the big bands of the Swing Era. You had to be good then or else."

Ol' Blue Eyes - Frank Sinatra.

"Picking the top female singer of the century, with respect to popular music, is much more difficult than the male counterpart. (The female singers) are more prolific and the overall standard I would say is higher." He prefers singers with a jazz background and therefore his choices were Billie Holiday, Ella Fitzgerald, Sarah Vaughan, Lena Horne and Peggy Lee.

Bill Wood of Leicester Forest East: "My choice for Best Female Singer of the Century is Edith Piaf, the 'little sparrow'. Shirley Bassey is overrated, Celine Dion is too strident. Diana Ross is rubbish as are Barbra Streisand, Ella Fitzgerald, Madonna, Doris Day, Whitney Houston – all rubbish!"

Mr. W.R. Jarvis of Leicester: "I am 71 and I must thank Frank Sinatra for giving me 57 years of pleasure during my life in his career from 1941 to 1998. He was the greatest entertainer, the best singer and a fine actor."

Cecilia Physick of Leicester: "My top choice for Male Pop Singer of the Century is Frank Sinatra and my second choice is Elvis Presley."

Jeff Toon, Leicester: "My vote is for Elvis Presley, The King. All the other male singers nominated have talent and merit a place in the list of popular singers but Elvis Presley's voice made me tingle from head to toe."

Top right: Shirley Bassey in 1971.
Top left: Elvis Presley in Love Me Tender. (photo courtesy BBC);
Centre: Cliff Richard in 1980 (photo from Leicester Mercury)
Bottom left: Paul McCartney supports the Leicester Arts Festival in 1968. (photo from Leicester Mercury.)

Barbra Streisand in 1994 (Photo courtesy BBC)

Gloria Barwell, Market Bosworth: "For me, Elvis is the King. I have been a fan since I was 13 years old. His music, to me, will live on. My dream is to go to Graceland (the Elvis Museum in Nashville, Tennessee). I hope one day my dream will come true. I like him not only for his singing but also for his films."

Tina Middleton, Braunstone Town, Leics: "My top choice is Cliff Richard. He has stayed true to his fans. He is a perfect gent and the man of my dreams."

Barry Goodacre, Loughborough, Leics: "My top choice is Dick Haymes. I'm not sure how performers like Michael Jackson and Mick Jagger can be considered singers at all. The technique of singing, judging by today's top male pop stars, seems to be a lost art."

Emma Henson of Humberstone, Leicester, says, "My top choice definitely is Elton John. He has been around for nearly thirty years and is still very popular. He holds the title of selling the most copies of a single but most of all, he has the most lovely voice and, if his voice has touched a 16-year-old-girl (me) then he should definitely be elected."

Mrs. P. Smith of Leicestershire commented: "In my opinion there is not another singer who comes close to Frank Sinatra. There will never be another one like him. He made every song he sang his own. What an entertainer!"

S. Bassett of Leicestershire: "My top choice is Elvis Presley for his good looks, singing and for changing musical history. My second choice is Cliff Richard for copying Elvis and ending up a star in his own right. I also like Howard Keel, John Lennon and Tom Jones."

W.R. Parker of Leicester rates Mario Lanza at the very top for having an operatic voice and also being a pop singer. The greatest pop singers, including Elvis and Sinatra, were fans of his, along with the great tenors of the century, he says.

Above, from top: Cleo Laine in 1982; Liza Minnelli in Stepping Out (1991, Paramount Pictures)**; Sarah Brightman; Debbie Harry, of Blondie.**

Chapter Eleven
Champions of Your Century : 1900 – 1999
POETS

From top: T. S. Eliot;
John Betjeman (Photo by Jane Bown, Camera Press)
Rudyard Kipling aged 22. (photo: PA)
Dannie Abse. (Photo courtesy of Dannie Abse)

When you enter the dining car of the London to Leicester train you never know who your travelling companion will turn out to be. I located the only vacant seat and found I was sitting opposite a prosperous executive who was engrossed in reading the back page of his newspaper. Angrily he tossed it aside.

"It's all very depressing," he said.

"Is it?"

"Yes, the sports results, the markets, and look at the weather."

I tried to cheer him up. "The weather's not perfect but Britain is a great place to live. Everyone agrees we have the world's best novelists, poets, cricket players and footballers."

He thought about it for a moment and then laughed. "Well, I suppose two out of four is not bad."

He preferred not to talk about sports at the moment. But as for literature, ah, that was something quite encouraging.

"You take Dylan Thomas, for example. Our family have enjoyed listening to his records for years. And we have read aloud many poems by Eliot, Auden, Betjeman, Larkin, Spender, Kipling and Rupert Brooke. Yes, it's great to be British."

I then asked the question I have been asking all my life. "Among all these poets, who do you think is the greatest?"

He shrugged. "I like so many. I think you should ask an expert."

Taking his advice I later put the question to Nicholas Everett of the English Department, University of

Leicester, who specialises in poetry from many countries.

This would help to round out the contenders because the question really is: Who is the Greatest Poet in the World in this Century?

Here is his international list of top contenders.

T.S. Eliot. "The Waste Land, written in 1922, is the most influential, most taught poem of the Century."

Thomas Hardy. (active at the turn of the Century). "He is the supreme English lyricist. He has written hardly any poems that don't work."

W.B. Yeats. Irish poet. "He has an amazing range. He redefined himself mid-career as a modern poet and succeeded in being thoroughly modern without breaking form."

W.H. Auden. "His works, Poems (1930 and 1933) and The Orators (1932) are still among the most exciting English poetry of the Century. He had a great range over a long career."

John Ashbery. American. "A New York poet who is one of the first to break this Century's image/compression fetish with complete success. His work is very expansive/very funny."

His additional selections are:

6. Wallace Stevens, American; 7. Philip Larkin, British; 8. Elizabeth Bishop, American; 9. Les Murray, Australian; and 10. Robert Lowell, American.

"But, of course ," he said, "The list could have consisted of a completely different line-up, such as: William Carlos Williams, Ezra Pound, Robert Frost, Seamus Heaney, John Betjeman, Edward Thomas, Geoffrey Hill, Marianne Moore, Stevie Smith and Sylvia Plath. And no doubt another ten have strong claims as well," he said.

Well-launched into the topic I asked many other people for their choices and got a number of

Philip Larkin, who at one time was on the staff at Leicester University Library, was awarded an honorary degree by the University in 1970. (photo from Leicester Mercury)

interesting candidates including Roger McGough, Ted Hughes, Dannie Abse, Jenny Joseph and Margaret Atwood.

Eventually, with the help of your nomination votes, we were able to draw up a list of the top contenders. They are, in alphabetical order:

Dannie Abse: This Cardiff poet has often given readings in Leicestershire and is well-known in local literary circles. He is the author of the brilliant love poem, Epithalamian.

W.H. Auden: In the pre-war era he was considered a certainty for the title of the greatest poet of the Half Century. The war changed many things, including attitudes towards poetry. He continues to be highly respected although his academic style is no longer in vogue.

John Betjeman: A people's poet who rose to the heights of Poet Laureate. He was seen as a strong force in making poetry accessible to everyone.

T.S. Eliot: His passion for change exactly met the mood of the post-war era. His versatility is enormous, from the epic poem, The Waste Land, to his current best-seller, Jellico Cats, the basis for the West End musical by Andrew Lloyd Webber.

Rudyard Kipling: A folk hero from the early years of the Century, he will always be associated with his poem (that became a song) On The Road to Mandalay.

Phillip Larkin: At the height of his career he was popular and highly respected. However, to some people he was later seen as an elitist at a time when it was out of fashion.

Sylvia Plath: More famous for her personal life than her poetry. Her suicide after being rejected by her lover struck a responsive chord in all quarters of the English-speaking world.

Stevie Smith: Her poem, Not Waving But Drowning, will always be quoted in English literature. Her career was greatly helped by her brilliant speaking voice that could captivate large audiences. Some critics took the view she could get applause reciting anything, including the telephone book. Some of her work was clearly of a high quality.

Dylan Thomas: The master of performance, he could also write with a touch of genius. The poems were great but it will always be the incredible voice that will be remembered by his fans.

W.B. Yeats: His talent assures a high place in literature despite the controversies of politics. He appears on everybody's list of the top poets of the Century.

Poets just missing the top ten were: Seamus Heaney, Rupert Brooke, Roger McGough, Ted Hughes, Thomas Hardy and Pam Ayres.

Chapter Twelve
Champions of Your Century : 1900 – 1999
NOVELISTS

Exactly half a Century ago, the famous American writer, John Steinbeck, called a news conference to declare: "The novel, as we know it, is finished as a major force in our society."

He said the cinema and the new media giant, television, would reduce novelists to screenwriters. Novels would be viewed only as possible scripts for TV or the movies. He may have been thinking of his own career, where the film of his novel, The Grapes of Wrath, had made him twenty times more famous than the book could have done.

However, as usual with such pronouncements about the future, he was half right and half wrong.

The novel no longer reigns supreme. But it is certainly not finished. In fact it is alive and well and flourishing everywhere.

Which brings us to our next category. Of all the great authors in many countries, who is the World's Outstanding Novelist of the Century?

For contenders we have looked to two major sources.

Here in Britain, in 1997, Waterstone's commissioned a public

Top left: Ernest Hemingway (photo from Camera Press);
Top right: Catherine Cookson (Photo from Camera Press); **Bottom right:**
George Orwell (photo courtesy BBC); **Bottom left: Graham Greene.**

**Local favourites –
Above left: Lynda Page;
Above right: Sue Townsend.**
(photos from Leicester Mercury.)

opinion survey to find out what books the people liked, regardless of how the critics rated them.

The survey produced the follow top ten list of writers and their most popular novel.

In order: J.R.R. Tolkien (The Lord of the Rings), George Orwell (Nineteen Eighty-Four), James Joyce (Ulysses), Joseph Heller (Catch 22), J.D. Salinger (The Catcher in the Rye), Harper Lee (To Kill a Mockingbird), Gabriel Garcia Marquez (One Hundred Years of Solitude), John Steinbeck (The Grapes of Wrath), Irvine Welsh (Trainspotting), Jung Chang (Wild Swans).

Other novelists in their top twenty-five included: F. Scott Fitzgerald, William Golding, Jack Kerouac, Aldous Huxley, Kenneth Grahame, A.A. Milne, Alice Walker, Albert Camus, C.S. Lewis, Franz Kafka and Margaret Mitchell, author of Gone With the Wind.

More recently this list was revised by Shona McGlashan, assistant manger of the Waterstone's branch in Leicester, to reflect the actual book sales and comments of customers in the Leicestershire area.

She said that locally Tolkien is only fourth among the favourite novelists.

"At the top is Helen Fielding, author of Bridget Jones' Diary and Cause Celeb. She has even had an evening of television programmes dedicated to her.

"Second in Leicestershire is Irvine Welsh, author of Trainspotting. I think he deserves a prize for getting so many people to read books who wouldn't otherwise have bothered.

"Third in the Leicestershire area is Bernard Cornwall, author of the Sharpe novels, who pushed Tolkien into fourth place locally. Fifth is the very successful local writer Lynda Page.

"Another local favourite in the top twenty is Leicestershire writer Sue Townsend, plus international writers Catherine Cookson, Meera Syal (whose novel was set in the Midlands), Mary Wesley and Joanna Trollope.

"Otherwise, the Leicester favourites generally followed the national trend."

Meanwhile, in America the Random House book publishers hired a team of experts to examine the claims of authors from all countries of the world, including Russia, to find the best novels of the Century, written in English.

The Random House team of literary critics selected this top ten list of novelists. They are (in order):

James Joyce, F. Scott Fitzgerald, Vladimir Nabokov, Aldous Huxley, William Faulkner, Joseph Heller, Arthur Koestler, D.H. Lawrence, John Steinbeck and Malcolm Lowry.

(This means they believe that the outstanding British novelist of the Century is Aldous Huxley, followed in second place by D.H. Lawrence, with Malcolm Lowry third).

Their top twenty includes George Orwell, Robert Graves and Virginia Woolf.

Away down in 45th place in the American survey is Ernest Hemingway, with The Sun Also Rises. Anthony Burgess is in 65th position.

With your help we were, at last, able to reach a consensus on the list of top ten finalists for the title of greatest novelist of the Century. .

Among five of the finalists, voters clearly indicated the book that most influenced their choices. D.H. Lawrence (Sons and Lovers), John Steinbeck (Grapes of Wrath), George Orwell (1984), James Joyce (Ulysses) and Ernest Hemingway (The Sun Also Rises).

For the remaining five, no specific novel was clearly indicated. Thomas Hardy, C.S. Lewis, Virginia Woolf, Catherine Cookson and Graham Greene.

Just missing the top ten were: Aldous Huxley, H.G. Wells, Anthony Burgess, Malcolm Lowry, Joseph Conrad and Henry James.

Poets and Novelists: What You Said

Dennis Stevenson of Melton Mowbray: "These are only my personal choices and are not based on the technical ability or merit of the writers. The people I have chosen have all contributed at least one work that has made a permanent impact on me.

"My selections for top novelists are: 1. D.H. Lawrence, 2. Ernest Hemingway, 3. George Orwell, 4. Malcolm Lowry and 5. Catherine Cookson.

"My selections for top poets are: 1. Rudyard Kipling, 2. T.S. Eliot, 3. Dylan Thomas, 4. John Betjeman and 5. Pam Ayres."

Ray Blakesley of Groby: "For a good read it has to be Rudyard Kipling, who holds the attention probably better than anyone else.

"I did not understand modern poetry until I read Sylvia Plath. I then realised how controlled her 'free' verse is, often with subtleties of rhyme which may not be apparent at first sight.

"For the use of language, which I may not always understand but which is marvellous read aloud, I admire Dylan Thomas; and another Welshman, just for pleasure, style and opinion, Dannie Abse."

Norman Harrington of Rothley: "John Betjeman isn't regarded as a profound poet but I have enjoyed much of his work.

"If the question is the best of the Century, I am not a critic and have not read sufficiently to say which are the best poets but from what I have gathered from reading and listening to experts, the consensus seems to be something like this:

D.H. Lawrence. (Photo courtesy Nottingham Evening Post)

Clockwise from top left:
W. H. Auden in 1970 (Photo by Peter Mitchell, Camera Press);
Drawing of Rupert Brooke;
Dylan Thomas (Photo courtesy of Reg Evans of Bridgend);
W.B. Yeats.

Poetry Monthly editor Martin Holroyd writes that the question of who is the best poet must be related to "which poet wrote the finest poem of this Century?

"Taking poetic craft as a pre-requisite, for me Dylan Thomas leads with Poem in October with its simple but cleverly constructed euphony; followed by Dannie Abse's love poem, Epithalamian.

"Stevie Smith's Not Waving But Drowning says much in a simple but direct manner and, in my scheme of things, is a definite third.

"John Betjeman's Upper Lamborne runs a solid fourth while Philip Larkin's Church Going must be placed as it considers the greatest questions that humankind has ever asked.

"Even if a poem is not remembered word for word; when it enters the individual's mind and stays there, the poem has done its job."

Heather Chandler of Ashby-de-la-Zouch writes: "My votes for the top five poets of the Century are as follows:

"1. Rupert Brooke, ever my favourite since my schooldays; 2. John Betjeman, a captivating personality I discovered more recently with a delightful and

"1. W.B. Yeats, 2. TS Eliot, 3. W.H. Auden, 4. Seamus Heaney, 5. Sylvia Plath, 6. Ted Hughes, 7. Thomas Hardy, 8. Philip Larkin and 9 Les Murray.

"For novelists, I suppose the scholarly selection would be:

"1. Thomas Hardy, 2. D.H. Lawrence, 3. James Joyce, 4. George Orwell, 5. Joseph Conrad, 6. Virginia Woolf, 7. Henry James, 8. H.G. Wells, 9 Graham Greene and 10 Anthony Burgess."

Far left: James Joyce in 1929; Left: Virginia Woolf.

Below: Roger McGough at a poetry reading in 1974 at Leicester Polytechnic (now De Montfort University).
(Picture from Leicester Mercury.)

sometimes quirky view of the world; 3. T.S. Eliot, who must be remembered if only for CATS; 4. Walter de la Mare, Another childhood favourite; and 5. Laurence Binyon, his poignant words are spoken every year at the time of Remembrance (and at all Legion meetings).

"Others who began to weave their magic in my schooldays were: Belloc, Chesterton, Kipling, Owen, Masefield, Sassoon and Yeats and I have since learnt to enjoy W.H. Auden, Wendy Cope, Elizabeth Jennings, Roger McGough and Dylan Thomas."

Julia Power of Groby: "My vote for the top poet of the century goes to Sir John Betjeman.

"Others I enjoy include Dylan Thomas and W.H. Auden".

Chapter Thirteen
Champions of Your Century : 1900 – 1999
CINEMA STARS

I met an American at a party who was going on and on about Elizabeth Taylor.

"England isn't the only country with a royal family, you know. We have our own royalty. In every sense of the word Elizabeth Taylor is like a queen to us."

I countered with, "Yes, but…"

There was no stopping him. "For a time Richard Burton was like a king in America. And then there's Cary Grant. I've always thought of him as a prince. It's the same thing. We have our own royal family."

I finally got a chance. "There's just one small problem. Your American royal family is all British. Elizabeth Taylor and Cary Grant were born and raised in England and, of course, Richard Burton was from Wales."

He nodded. "Yes, that's true. But, then, everyone knows we import many of our best things from Britain."

It was a handsome admission. I responded in the same spirit.

"However, your main point is absolutely right. For most of this Century, your top cinema stars have been very much like a royal family for America."

He was all smiles. It was clear the special relationship between Britain and America had been preserved. He even offered to buy me a drink.

From Top:
Ingrid Bergman plays Gladys Aylwood in *The Inn of the Sixth Happiness* (20th Century Fox) (photo courtesy BBC);
Meryl Streep in *The French Lieutenant's Woman* (1981, United Artists);
Vivien Leigh as Scarlett O'Hara in *Gone With The Wind* (1939, Selznick Int'l Pictures);
Marilyn Monroe, in her unfinished film *Something's Got to Give* (20th Century Fox);
Greta Garbo in *Grand Hotel* (Picture from Granada Television).

Top left: Richard Burton (left) and Peter O'Toole in *Becket* (1964, Paramount Pictures);
Top right: Humphrey Bogart in The African Queen (1951, Horizon Films/Carlton International Media Ltd);
Bottom: Harrison Ford as Han Solo in *Star Wars* (1977, Star Wars Productions).

I decided not to disturb the happy moment by adding that the era he was describing had gone with the wind. For the first half of the Century Hollywood was supreme.

After the Second World War, however, there were thousands of new celebrities from television, sports, singing and the world of fashion. The American royal family of celebrities now is so large it may soon outnumber the rest of the population.

At the same time, just ever so slightly, the impact of cinema stars is beginning to fade.

But our main purpose is not to look to the future but to review the past.

And it was glorious.

In this spirit we began the search for the outstanding cinema stars of the Century.

The most interesting factor in the list of male actors is that the performers with the fewest Oscars appeared to be the most popular.

Richard Burton has a wide following but never won an Academy Award in his life. Sean Connery is an international superstar but won his only oscar late in his career in a supporting role.

Cary Grant is in everyone's list of top five cinema actors but his only award was an honorary one when he retired.

Humphrey Bogart had an immense following during the war, especially after his starring role in Casablanca, but didn't win an Oscar until late in life in The African Queen.

From top left: John Wayne in *El Dorado* (1967, Paramount Pictures); **Clint Eastwood** in *Bronco Billy* (Photo Courtesy BBC); **Marlon Brando** as *The Godfather* (1972, Paramount Pictures); **Charlton Heston** in *Ben Hur* (1959, MGM); **Yul Brynner** in *The King and I* (1956, 20th Century Fox); **Orson Welles** in *Citizen Kane* (1941, RKO Radio Pictures).

From top right: Susan Hayward (photo courtesy United Artists, 1958); **Joan Crawford** in 1957; **Greer Garson** as Queen Mary in *The Abdication of Edward VIII*; **Betty Grable** in *Wabash Avenue* (1950, 20th Century Fox); **and Jane Fonda** in *Coming Home* (1978, United Artists).

Other box office favourites with few awards included Sidney Poitier, Charlton Heston, Alec Guinness, Ronald Colman, James Cagney, James Stewart, Gary Cooper, Henry Fonda and Clark Gable.

The moral of the story seems to be that Hollywood doesn't always get it right.

In any case, there are many additional candidates for the title of the greatest cinema actor of the Century. From Britain: Laurence Olivier, Anthony Hopkins, Jeremy Irons, Michael Caine, Ben Kingsley, Hugh Grant and Kenneth Brannagh.

Further candidates from America include: Harrison Ford, Gregory Peck, Dustin Hoffman, Jack Nicholson, Spencer Tracy, Marlon Brando, Tom Cruise, Robert Redford, Burt Lancaster, Jack Lemmon, John Wayne, Robert Mitchum and William Holden.

Unlike the men, the most popular cinema actresses of the Century tended to have a long list of Academy Award nominations.

Katharine Hepburn won four Oscars on ten nominations, Bette Davis had two on ten nominations, Meryl Streep had two for nine and Geraldine Page one for eight.

Those with seven nominations were Ingrid Bergman, Jane Fonda and Greer Garson while Deborah Kerr had six.

Following with five each were Elizabeth Taylor, Audrey Hepburn, Anne Bancroft, Olivia de Havilland, Susan Hayward, Shirley MacLaine, Vanessa Redgrave and Maggie Smith.

Other fan favourites who won Oscars include Glenda Jackson and Vivien Leigh.

And then there was Marilyn Monroe. She never won an award but her spectacular and ultimately

From top: Michael Caine and Laurence Olivier in Sleuth (1972, Palomar Pictures)**;**
Sean Connery as a Soviet submarine captain in The Hunt For Red October. (1990, Paramount Pictures);
James Stewart in Dear Brigitte (1965, 20th Century Fox, directed by Henry Koster)**;**
Anthony Hopkins and Anthony Heald in The Silence of the Lambs (1991, Orion Pictures Corp./MGM Turner)**;**

tragic life caught the attention of millions of people and she has become one of the most popular cinema stars of the Century.

Decision day was always going to be tough, given the strong list of candidates. Major contenders who just missed the final ten were: Bette Davis, Greta Garbo, Julia Roberts, Jane Fonda, Susan Hayward and Shirley MacLaine.

Film Stars: What You Said

Trudy Cameron of Leicestershire: "My top choice is Robert Mitchum. He was under-rated because he was such an easy-going actor. He was also a very considerate actor to work with and was helpful to the rest of the cast. My other favourites are Cary Grant, James Stewart and Michael Caine."

Marilyn Monroe caught the attention of early voters in the category of Best Female Cinema Star of the Century. Also doing well were Ingrid Bergman, Katharine Hepburn, Meryl Streep and Kate Winslet.

N. Preston of Leicestershire writes: "Marilyn Monroe was my idol. She really was beautiful. I also support Meryl Streep for her acting. She can take any part."

Sarah-Kay of Fleckney, Leics: "I feel Marilyn Monroe should win because, along with her goddess looks, she brought a whole new meaning to the word feminine. Her achievement of moving from pauper to princess has inspired millions, me being one of them. I am only seventeen but I have been a dedicated fan for four years and she has helped me become what I am now."

David Fitzhugh of Leicester: "Elizabeth Taylor is a really incredible talent. Loved all her films, especially those with Richard Burton. Audrey Hepburn was also a great talent and a caring and sincere

Top: Richard Burton and Elizabeth Taylor in *Cleopatra*. (1963, 20th Century Fox.)
Middle: Humphrey Bogart and Katharine Hepburn in *The African Queen*. (1951, Horizon Films/Carlton International Media Ltd)
Right: Audrey Hepburn and Fred Astaire in *Funny Face*. (1957, Paramount Pictures)

human being. Marilyn Monroe cuts a tragic figure. She was not that talented but she worked hard on her roles. Others I support are Hayley Mills, Rita Tushingham and especially the silent film star, Louise Brooks. To me she had everything, beauty talent and poise.

"My vote for best actor of the Century has to be Jimmy Cagney. I love all his films. There was something about Jimmy Cagney that makes him stand out against all the contenders. Richard Burton comes a close second. He was pure brilliance.

"I also liked Michael Caine and Marlon Brando but not Cary Grant and I didn't find John Wayne that interesting although he made some good films. As for the modern actors, real talent is missing. They are just five-minute wonders."

Trudy Cameron of Braunstone: "My top choice is Ingrid Bergman followed by Katharine Hepburn, Bette Davis, Deborah Kerr and Julia Roberts."

C. Fraser of Market Harborough: "My first choice is Katharine Hepburn. Second is Meryl Streep, she is beautiful, multi-talented and so versatile. I also liked Susan Hayward, she was beautiful, talented and had a fantastic voice."

Miss L. Smith of Loughborough: "I am 20 years old and my top choice is Kate Winslet. Watching good actresses like her makes me proud to be British."

John Challis of Melton Mowbray: "As much as I have enjoyed the acting talents of Bette Davis, Katharine Hepburn, Barbara Stanwyck and Barbra Streisand, my vote for title would have to go to Meryl Streep for the various characters she has played most convincingly down the years.

"I could write a long list of male screen actors for the title of cinema actor of the Century but after due consideration my vote is for the actor's actor, Spencer Tracy."

Top: Leonardo DiCaprio and Kate Winslet in Titanic. (1997, 20th Century Fox)
Bottom: Gladys Cooper (left) and Deborah Kerr (right) in *Separate Tables* (1958, Hecht, Hill and Lancaster)

PART TWO:

THE CHAMPIONS OF YOUR CENTURY
1900-1999

"And here are the results..."

Chapter Fourteen
Champions of Your Century : 1900 – 1999

GREATEST CINEMA STARS, MALE and FEMALE

Scottish superstar Sean Connery has been voted the greatest cinema actor of the Century. Swedish actress Ingrid Bergman has been named the greatest female cinema perfomer.

Connery made his reputation as James Bond, a character his Japanese fans called "Kiss-kiss, bang-bang."

He saw off strong challenges from Harrison Ford, Anthony Hopkins and Cary Grant to win the title.

Cary Grant was the top contender from England and the only one of the top four to have been in films in both the first and second half of the century.

Connery is from Scotland, Harrison Ford from America and Anthony Hopkins from Wales.

For the female contenders, right from the beginning it was a two-way contest between Casablanca star Ingrid Bergman and Katharine Hepburn, who has won more awards than any other actress. Both made a strong impact in the 1930s and for many years thereafter.

While six of the ten finalists are British, only one, Audrey Hepburn, who is of English and Dutch parentage, made the top three.

By contrast with the men, no actress currently active in films made the top five, bearing out the contention of Meryl Streep that the dominance of action movies means there are few good roles for women in the cinema any more.

The Titanic star, Kate Winslet, was the most popular of active performers while Streep finished seventh.

It was also interesting to note that, while Ingrid Bergman benefited greatly by the continuing popularity of Casablanca, the attitude towards her co-star, Humphrey Bogart is mixed. In the nomination round,

Above: Sean Connery with Christan Slater in *The Name of the Rose* (1986, ZDF/20th Century Fox)

Champions of Your Century 1900 – 1999
GREATEST CINEMA ACTOR

1	Sean Connery	623 votes
2	Harrison Ford	591 votes
3	Anthony Hopkins	587 votes
4	Cary Grant	538 votes
5	James Stewart	363 votes
6	Humphrey Bogart	322 votes
7	Richard Burton	316 votes
8	Michael Caine	289 votes
9	James Cagney	106 votes
10	Clark Gable	102 votes

voters said Bogart was magic in Casablanca but they didn't like his earlier gangster films and so they were undecided about where to rank him.

Meanwhile, the two stars of the classic film, Gone With the Wind, Clark Gable and Vivien Leigh, fared badly in the final round of voting. A number of readers had said they felt the film was larger than any of the actors, although they felt Vivien Leigh definitely earned her Academy Award.

Photos: Above: Sean Connery as King Arthur in First Knight, 1995, Columbia Pictures; Harrison Ford - Star Wars, 1977, 20th Century Fox; Anthony Hopkins - Shadowlands, 1993, Shadowlands Productions; Cary Grant - To Catch a Thief, 1953, United Artists; James Stewart - Universal-International Films of America; Humphrey Bogart in The African Queen, 1951, Horizon Films; Richard Burton - Becket, 1964, Paramount Pictures; Michael Caine - Hannah and Her Sisters, 1986, Orion Pictures; James Cagney.

Right: Sean Connery as James Bond, in Diamonds are Forever (1971, Danjaq Productions/MGM).

Champions of Your Century 1900 – 1999
GREATEST CINEMA ACTRESS

1	Ingrid Bergman	724 votes
2	Katharine Hepburn	615 votes
3	Audrey Hepburn	389 votes
4	Elizabeth Taylor	320 votes
5	Marilyn Monroe	303 votes
6	Kate Winslet	302 votes
7	Meryl Streep	288 votes
8	Vivien Leigh	237 votes
9	Glenda Jackson	221 votes
10	Deborah Kerr	128 votes

Photos: Ingrid Bergman - The Inn of the Sixth Happiness, 1958, 20th Century Fox, photo courtesy BBC; Katherine Hepburn - photo courtesy BBC; Audrey Hepburn - My Fair Lady, 1964, Warner Bros.; Elizabeth Taylor - Taming of the Shrew, 1967, Columbia Pictures; Marilyn Munroe - Something's Got To Give, 20th Century Fox.; Kate Winslet - Titanic, 1997, 20th Century Fox; Meryl Streep - The French Lieutenant's Woman, 1981, United Artists; Vivien Leigh - Gone with the Wind, 1939, Selznick Int'l Pictures; Glenda Jackson in Hopscotch, 1980, AVCO Embassy Pictures; Deborah Kerr - Separate Tables, 1958, Hecht, Hill & Lancaster.

"You must remember this." Ingrid Bergman has been voted the champion film actress of the Century for her brilliant roles in Anastasia, Inn of the Sixth Happiness, For Whom the Bell Tolls and, of course, Casablanca, proving once again the world will always welcome lovers as time goes by. (Photo from Anastasia, 1956, 20th Century Fox.)

Chapter Fifteen
Champions of Your Century : 1900 – 1999
GREATEST BREED OF DOG and GREATEST NOVELIST

The Golden Retriever has been voted the outstanding dog breed of the Century. It easily topped the poll with 1,029 votes. The Labrador was second with 727.

The Border Collie, German Shepherd and West Highland Terrier also made a strong showing.

Meanwhile, the title of best novelist of the Century went to D.H. Lawrence. George Orwell was second and James Joyce came third.

For the novelists, Lawrence was supported both by the university community and the general public. The Nottinghamshire writer was often controversial but for years he has been recognised as a major literary talent.

The continuing popularity of the novel 1984 helped to propel Orwell into second place. James Joyce won wide support from literary scholars but his books are regarded as a bit obscure by many general readers.

The victory by the Golden Retriever breed came as no surprise to Maureen Ward, Secretary of the Leicester City Canine Society.

"The Golden Retriever is a lovely all around family pet, very good with children. It is gentle and sensitive and very responsive."

She said they are often used in television adverts because they are intelligent and also easy to work with, very patient.

"One of the things I like best about them is they are always cheerful."

Hamlet, a Golden Retriever from Medbourne takes a celebratory dip.

In recent years the breed has also been used more and more as guide dogs.

"The Labrador is popular because it is very similar in nature and makes an excellent pet. They are also working dogs, highly regarded for being able to sniff out drugs. They have very remarkable noses."

She said the Border Collie is well known as an excellent working dog, responsive to commands. In recent years they have grown in popularity as show dogs as well.

"They can be excellent family dogs. Sometimes they will herd young children together to protect them from any danger. They are very loyal."

She said the German Shepherd is a beautiful dog and top rated for guard duty and police work. In recent years it has been less popular as a family dog because of a few unfortunate incidents which are not always the dog's fault, she said.

She said the West Highland Terrier is a delightful dog but it can surprise you by being a bit more lively than you might expect.

"It's like the dog is saying, I may only be little, but deep down I'm big! I think I would describe them as being a cocky dog but they are very affectionate."

Champions of Your Century 1900 – 1999
BEST BREED OF DOG

1	Golden Retriever	1,029 votes
2	Labrador	727 votes
3	Border Collie	439 votes
4	German Shepherd	407 votes
5	West Highland Terrier	258 votes
6	English Springer Spaniel	212 votes
7	Yorkshire Terrier	176 votes
8	Old English Sheepdog	175 votes
9	St. Bernard	145 votes
10	Dachshund	57 votes

Champions of Your Century 1900 – 1999

GREATEST NOVELIST

1	D. H. Lawrence	711 votes
2	George Orwell	443 votes
3	James Joyce	362 votes
4	Ernest Hemingway	234 votes
5	Thomas Hardy	203 votes
6	Catherine Cookson	201 votes
7	C. S. Lewis	197 votes
8	Graham Greene	146 votes
9	John Steinbeck	126 votes
10	Virginia Woolf	102 votes

Chapter Sixteen
Champions of Your Century : 1900 – 1999

GREATEST COMEDY TEAM and GREATEST WAR SONG

Morecambe and Wise have been elected the Greatest Comedy Team of the Century.

Second was the Fawlty Towers team of John Cleese, Prunella Scales, Andrew Sachs and Connie Booth. The Two Ronnies and French and Saunders were tied in third place.

We'll Meet Again was voted the greatest song of the war years, closely followed by The White Cliffs of Dover. Both were made famous by Vera Lynn.

The Glenn Miller swing tune, In The Mood, was third.

In a sense, Morecambe and Wise had already been acknowledged as the best ever in 1977 when about half the population of Britain watched their Christmas special. They continued to be television favourites for many years.

The election surprise was the strength of the Fawlty Towers team, based on the votes of young admirers. They almost pulled off the upset of the Century.

Fans of Fawlty Towers were helped by re-runs of the television series and by the continuing popularity of John (Basil) Cleese and Prunella (Sybil) Scales and by fond memories of Andrew Sachs as Manuel and Connie Booth as Polly.

Young voters also propelled Monty Python into fifth place.

The decisive factor in the election was that Morecambe and Wise won support among all age groups, coming first in most cases and coming at least second among young voters.

The Two Ronnies and French and Saunders were strong challengers throughout the voting.

Film favourites, The Marx Brothers and Laurel and Hardy, did well but British teams from the past, The Goon Show and Les Dawson and Roy Barraclough, had less support than expected.

As for the greatest songs of the war years, it was a close contest between the two great Vera Lynn classics, We'll Meet Again and The White Cliffs of Dover. Both became anthems of determination during the war.

The Glenn Miller military band from America brought In The Mood

Eric Morcambe and Ernie Wise. *(Photo Courtesy BBC.)*

Champions of Your Century 1900 – 1999
GREATEST COMEDY TEAM

1	Morecambe and Wise	877 votes
2	Fawlty Towers	642 votes
3	The Two Ronnies	476 votes
3	French and Saunders	476 votes
5	Monty Python	407 votes
6	Laurel and Hardy	322 votes
7	The Marx Brothers	279 votes
8	Bob Hope and Bing Crosby	276 votes
9	The Goon Show	215 votes
10	Dawson & Barraclough	106 votes

and other songs to Britain to raise the morale of American troops. Many British teenagers fell in love to the music and came to regard In The Mood as their special song.

There was a respectable showing by the two British singing comedians of the war years who were film stars of the era. Gracie Fields finished fourth with Wish Me Luck as You Wave Me Goodbye and George Formby was sixth with his classic song, Leaning On a Lamp Post.

Photos: Morcambe and Wise, BBC; John Cleese - Fawlty Towers, BBC; The Two Ronnies, BBC, 1985; French and Saunders, BBC, 1987; Monty Python, BBC; Laurel and Hardy; The Marx Brothers, photo from BBC; The Goons, 1991; Dawson and Friends, Yorkshire Television, 1977, Pearson Library.

Right: Vera Lynn, who recorded many of the best loved songs of the second world war. (Photo BBC, 1969)

Photos below: Vera Lynn on ENSA duty; Glenn Miller; Gracie Fields; George Formby; Revellers on VE day 1945; a world war two Wellington bomber.

Champions of Your Century 1900 – 1999
BEST SONG OF THE WAR YEARS

1	**We'll Meet Again** (Charles/Parker)	875 votes
2	**The White Cliffs Of Dover** (Nat Burton/Walter Kent)	761 votes
3	**In The Mood** (Joe Garland/Andy Razaf)	432 votes
4	**Wish Me Luck As You Wave Me Goodbye** (Park/Parr/Davies)	186 votes
5	**I'll Be Seeing You** (Irving Kahal/Sammy Fain)	172 votes
6	**Leaning On A Lamp Post** (Noel Gay)	157 votes
7	**Roll Out The Barrel**	144 votes
8	**Keep The Home Fires Burning** (Ford/Novello)	135 votes
9	**Yours** (Jack Sherr/Gonzalo Roig)	42 votes
10	**Coming In On A Wing And A Prayer** (Adamson/McHugh)	41 votes

Chapter Seventeen
Champions of Your Century : 1900 – 1999

GREATEST ROCK GROUP and SPEAKING VOICE

The Beatles have been voted the Greatest Rock Group of the Century. They turned back a challenge from ABBA by a comfortable margin of 1,157 votes to 785. Queen was third with 472.

Meanwhile, Winston Churchill was voted to have the Greatest Speaking Voice of the Century but he was in a close race with the dynamic American civil rights leader Martin Luther King Jr. Richard Burton came third.

Neither victory could be called a surprise.

In preliminary surveys to find the top ten candidates for best rock group, the most common reply was, "You mean, besides The Beatles?"

Their widespread support was due not only to the quality of the band but also for their awesome achievement in 1964 of making Britain the world's capital for entertainment, taking the title away from America.

Many people said The Beatles made them feel good about being British, the equivalent of England's World Cup victory in 1966.

The Beatles, and the rest of the British invasion that followed, helped to rejuvenate the economy, made London the world's top tourist destination and created a golden glow that

The Beatles in 1963. A Leicester Mercury account at the time reported John Lennon (right) as liking the colour black and dark clothes, while Paul McCartney (left) included polo neck sweaters and Ray Charles on his list. (Photo from Leicester Mercury).

continues to this day.

ABBA, in second place, made a strong showing with voters of all ages. Queen also did well, especially with older rock fans. In the final week, The Bee Gees made a strong move to finish fourth, just ahead of Oasis.

Many people commented on the absence of the Rolling Stones from the list. During the nomination process many people said they had stopped being fans of the Stones because they had stayed around too long and seemed to have become almost a satire of themselves. If they had retired fifteen years ago they would almost certainly have made a strong showing in the top ten.

The big news in the category of

Winston Churchill. (Photo from Northcliffe Newspapers)

Champions of Your Century 1900 – 1999
GREATEST ROCK GROUP

1	The Beatles	1,157 votes
2	ABBA	785 votes
3	Queen	472 votes
4	The Bee Gees	351 votes
5	Oasis	327 votes
6	The Doors	228 votes
7	Bon Jovi	201 votes
8	The Beach Boys	183 votes
9	Showaddywaddy	102 votes
10	Aerosmith	79 votes

Greatest Speaking Voice was the widespread support among young people for Martin Luther King Jr. He actually came out in front of Churchill among voters under 20.

However, Churchill's very large support among adults gave him the victory.

Richard Burton did well, as expected. The Queen was a respectable fourth. Some voters rated her as, "not dynamic but an excellent speaker."

Dylan Thomas, considered to be the best performance poet of the Century, did not do as well as expected but it was a quality field and the competition was tough. For example, the highly-regarded actress Glenda Jackson finished ninth.

The message seemed to be, it was an achievement just to have made the top ten in this category.

Champions of Your Century 1900 – 1999
BEST SPEAKING VOICE

1	Winston Churchill	896 votes
2	Martin Luther King Jr.	804 votes
3	Richard Burton	459 votes
4	Queen Elizabeth II	242 votes
5	Laurence Olivier	176 votes
6	Mahatma Gandhi	153 votes
7	John F. Kennedy	137 votes
8	Dylan Thomas	84 votes
9	Glenda Jackson	73 votes
10	Franklin D. Roosevelt	41 votes

Chapter Eighteen
Champions of Your Century : 1900 – 1999

GREATEST MALE and FEMALE COMEDIANS

Benny Hill and Victoria Wood have been voted the greatest comedians of the Century.

Hill won in a close finish with Tommy Cooper, Bob Hope, Peter Sellers, Charlie Chaplin and Les Dawson. Earlier in the election, it looked like all ten candidates might end in a tie for first place. They almost did.

By contrast, Victoria Wood won in a landslide with 1,012 votes. Dawn French was second with 636 and her partner, Jennifer Saunders, came third with 541.

While Benny Hill is not to everyone's taste, he has a massive following around the world where his television shows are being re-run over and over again. He mastered the art of television comedy better than anyone in the Century.

Those who admired him spoke of his innocent little-boy qualities. Those who didn't admire him called some of his comedy routines crude.

By contrast, nobody had a bad word to say about Tommy Cooper. He might not have been the funniest but he seemed to be the most likeable comic of them all, according to our surveys.

British-born comedian, Bob Hope, won a very high rating here, coming third. America almost certainly will select him as their comedian of the Century, ahead of their other British import Charlie Chaplin.

Britain's top stand-up comedian of the first half century, Max Miller, did not have enough support from young voters to challenge for the title.

Victoria Wood was an easy winner among female comedians. She has been the greatest female stand-up comedian for many years and has also done well in television comedy dramas. She seems on the

Benny Hill and his 'Hill's Angels'.
(Thames Television, photo from Pearson Library)

Champions of Your Century 1900 – 1999
GREATEST MALE COMEDIAN

1	Benny Hill	467 votes
2	Tommy Cooper	458 votes
3	Bob Hope	422 votes
4	Peter Sellers	338 votes
5	Charlie Chaplin	334 votes
6	Les Dawson	321 votes
7	Ken Dodd	270 votes
8	Tony Hancock	266 votes
9	Max Miller	236 votes
10	Frankie Howerd	211 votes

threshold of becoming an icon of the Century.

Her main competition came from the comedy team of French and Saunders and from the cast of Absolutely Fabulous.

America's top female comedian Lucille Ball made a respectable showing, finishing just ahead of that Carry On girl Barbara Windsor and Gracie Fields, the comedy star of the pre-war era.

Fawlty Towers star Prunella Scales continues to be popular, due partly to her high profile in television adverts.

The only active male comedian in the Top Ten is Ken Dodd. The rest have retired or passed on.

We can only hope that the new Millennium will produce entertainers as good as these.

There are two reasons why Dodd draws a full house everywhere he appears. First, because he's good. Second, because he is the last representative of the male comedy giants of the Twentieth Century.

In our new Millennium the stand-up comic is virtually certain to disappear. There will be comedy actors in sitcoms and other television programmes but it won't be the same. It might be better, who knows, but it won't be the same.

We have been blessed with giants of comedy in the Twentieth Century and it's certain we will never see their like again.

If you do get a chance to see the last man, Ken Dodd, in person or on television, by all means do so. You will be watching the last artist of a great age.

As for the rest of them, thanks for the memories, it may well have been the greatest era for comedy in the history of the world.

Champions of Your Century 1900 – 1999
GREATEST FEMALE COMEDIANS

1	Victoria Wood	1,012 votes
2	Dawn French	636 votes
3	Jennifer Saunders	541 votes
4	Joanna Lumley	257 votes
5	Lucille Ball	232 votes
6	Barbara Windsor	219 votes
7	Gracie Fields	203 votes
8	Prunella Scales	116 votes
9	Maureen Lipman	63 votes
10	Joyce Grenfell	47 votes

Victoria Wood in 1993
(Photo courtesy BBC)

Chapter Nineteen
Champions of Your Century : 1900 – 1999
GREATEST MUSICAL and DISNEY ANIMATED FILMS

The Sound of Music has been elected the Outstanding Musical Film of the Century. The deciding factor may well have been the vision of Julie Andrews spinning around on a mountaintop before bursting into song.

It continues to be one of the most vivid film images of all time.

Voters also mentioned the memory of children dancing happily through Salzburg singing Do-Re-Mi.

Meanwhile, The Lion King was named the Best Disney Animated Film.

In both categories the generation gap played a key role.

People of all ages placed The Sound of Music first or second.

However, young people almost inevitably favoured the teenage romance, Grease, starring Olivia Newton-John and John Travolta.

The outcome was in doubt right up to the final week.

The films finished one-two in a very strong field. The Judy Garland classic, The Wizard of Oz, edged out the other Julie Andrews favourite, Mary Poppins, for third place.

For many years, organisations in America had been promoting Singin' in the Rain as the best musical of all time. It finished sixth in our poll.

One of the most compelling footnotes of the election is that My Fair Lady got almost no support at all among young voters, who considered it "quaint and old fashioned" but it still has many supporters among those over thirty.

The generation gap was also at work in the category of Best Disney Animated Film, but in a very gentle way.

The Von Trapp family escape over the mountains in *The Sound of Music*, (1965, 20th Century Fox)

Children under seven, and their mothers, have a love affair with The Jungle Book. Voters in Leicestershire say their infants respond favourably to the free-spirited bear, Baloo, singing about the Bare Necessities of Life.

One mother said her son, at only 18 months, loved the video so much he would stand up and get ready to march with the elephants as soon as he heard the first chord.

Another mother reported: "My son had to have a banana as soon as the monkeys in the film got theirs."

By contrast, The Lion King was unusual for a children's animated cartoon, being a sophisticated story of guilt and remorse. A youngster would have had to be at least 10 to fully understand the plot and the fast-moving jokes. Older children and adults loved the film, of course, and that was the key factor in its victory.

The irony is that in 1950 most major surveys selected Snow White and the Seven Dwarfs as the greatest Disney film of the Half Century in a very close contest with Bambi.

Film reviewers in that year said it would be up to the voters in 1999 to determine for all time which was the better Disney film of the Century.

Well, Snow White again finished ahead of Bambi but now it no longer matters. They were third and fourth in the final voting, behind the more recent productions, The Lion King and The Jungle Book.

Meanwhile, The Beauty and the Beast, the only Disney project to be nominated best film of the year, finished behind six other contenders.

Images continue to play a key role when it comes to remembering the past.

The Lady and The Tramp finished in fifth place in a strong field and yet few people can remember the story. However, they do remember the two dogs sharing a plate of spaghetti and, by accident, eating the same strand and coming together, inevitably, in a kiss.

It's amazing how a single image can knock out 101 Dalmatians, Beauty and the Beast, Dumbo, Pinocchio and Cinderella.

Champions of Your Century 1900 – 1999
TOP MUSICAL FILM

1	**The Sound of Music**	1965, 20th C. Fox, directed by Robert Wise	941 votes
2	**Grease**	1978, Paramount, directed by Randal Kleiser	617 votes
3	**The Wizard of Oz**	1939, MGM, directed by Victor Fleming	358 votes
4	**Mary Poppins**	1964, Walt Disney, directed by Robert Stevenson	347 votes
5	**West Side Story**	1961, United Artists, directed by Jerome Robbins & Robert Wise	338 votes
6	**Singin' in the Rain**	1952, MGM, directed by Stanley Donan & Gene Kelly	314 votes
7	**A Hard Day's Night**	1964, United Artistst, directed by Richard Lester	244 votes
8	**My Fair Lady**	1964, Warner Bros., directed by George Cukor	192 votes
9	**The King and I**	1956, 20th C. Fox, directed by Walter Lang	155 votes
10	**Gigi**	1958, MGM, directed by Vincente Minnelli	64 votes

Champions of Your Century 1900 – 1999
BEST DISNEY ANIMATED FILM

1	**The Lion King**		1,016 votes
2	**The Jungle Book**		615 votes
3	**Snow White** and the Seven Dwarfs		363 votes
4	**Bambi**		278 votes
5	**Lady and the Tramp**		271 votes
6	**101 Dalmatians**		245 votes
7	**Beauty and the Beast**		236 votes
8	**Dumbo**		205 votes
9	**Pinocchio**		193 votes
10	**Cinderella**		128 votes

Top: The Lion King. All pictures on this page © Walt Disney Productions

Chapter Twenty

Champions of Your Century : 1900 – 1999

GREATEST CINEMA FILM and GREATEST POET

Gone With The Wind has been crowned the greatest cinema film of the Century. Casablanca was second and there was a tie for third between Titanic and Shakespeare In Love.

The brilliant, innovative writer T.S. Eliot was a landslide winner for the title of the best poet of the Century.

In the films category, the top two could not be more unlike. GWTW came out in 1939 after three years of the most frenetic promotion in history.

Casablanca, on the other hand, was just one of several dozen movies being made in 1943 and nobody expected much of it. Quite simply, it was the right movie with the right message at the right time.

But the stage belongs to the champion.

Margaret Mitchell's novel about how the American Civil War brought an end to an era in the south had been a best-seller in 1936. David O. Selznick bought the rights and hyped the film for three years.

He succeeded in capturing the attention of the English-speaking world by promoting every stage of the film's development. His biggest success was provoking thousands of letters nominating various American stars to play the role of Scarlett O'Hara. It was generally agreed the American star must be from the south.

The winner, Vivien Leigh, came from the south, but not from the nation they expected.

However the real impact of the film became evident in Santa Barbara, a community north of Hollywood. The cinema theatres there often had signs reading only: New film premiere. It was all a great mystery.

In late 1939 there were long line-ups at every theatre in Santa Barbara hoping it would turn out to be Gone With The Wind. When the various films came on there were groans of disappointment.

Then, one evening, the film began with the announcement that David O. Selznick with MGM were pleased to present his Technicolor

Clark Gable and Vivien Leigh get passionate in *Gone With The Wind* (1939, Selznick International Pictures)

presentation of…..

And there was wave of applause in the audience but it was restrained because Selznick and MGM did many films together and then the next words were:

"Margaret Mitchell's story of the old south…"

There was a wave of cheering and then the theme music began and the first giant word appeared: GONE…

The theatre manager said this single word was greeted by the loudest scream he had ever heard in his life and when the other words followed: WITH THE WIND, the cheering shook the building like an earthquake.

He said the screams of joy continued through the lengthy credits and only subsided in time to hear Scarlett O'Hara say her first "Fiddle-dee-dee."

By and large the film matched its immense build-up. It was certainly a landmark production.

By contrast, Casablanca was a bit of magic that surprised everyone because not much was expected of it.

As it turned out, Casablanca also caused explosions of joy in the cinema theatres.

The time was 1943 and the world was at war.

Nazi Officer: "Are you one of those people who can not bear to see us in their beloved Paris?"

Bogart: "It's not particularly MY beloved Paris."

Nazi Officer: "Can you imagine us in London?"

Bogart: "When you get there, ask me!"

The applause rocked the theatre.

Two Oscar winners of the present decade ended in a tie for third. Shakespeare In Love is a great example of everything Britain is famous for: talent, brilliance, culture, humour. Titanic is a compelling drama with songs and special effects that were unsurpassed.

Champions of Your Century 1900 – 1999
BEST CINEMA FILM

1	**Gone with the Wind** 1939, Selznick International Pictures, directed by Victor Fleming		877 votes
2	**Casablanca** 1942, Warner Bros., directed by Michael Curtiz		642 votes
3	**Shakespeare in Love** 1998, Miramax, directed by John Madden		476 votes
3	**Titanic** 1997, 20th C. Fox, directed by James Cameron		476 votes
5	**Star Wars** 1977, 20th C. Fox, directed by George Lucas		407 votes
6	**Dr. Zhivago** 1965, MGM, directed by David Lean		322 votes
7	**Lawrence of Arabia** 1962, Columbia Pictures, directed by David Lean		279 votes
8	**Four Weddings and a Funeral** 1994, Polygram, directed by Mike Newell		276 votes
9	**Ben Hur** 1959, MGM, directed by William Wyler		215 votes
10	**Citizen Kane** 1941, RKO Radio Pictures, directed by Orson Welles		106 votes

This category had a splendid array of contenders and so it was inevitable that some great films, like Dr. Zhivago, Lawrence of Arabia and Four Weddings and a Funeral had to trail the field. Still, it was startling to see the much-honoured Ben Hur come only ninth.

However, there was no disputing the credentials of the top four.

The victory by T.S. Eliot was a tribute to his talent, his innovation, his great poem The Waste Land, and his continuing success in the popular culture because of his poem about cats which formed the basis for the Andrew Lloyd Webber musical.

He was supported by both the universities and the general public and was clearly the poet of the Century.

His contenders were three writers who are generally regarded as poets of the people and all highly talented: John Betjeman, Rudyard Kipling and Dylan Thomas.

Dylan, in particular, has a widespread fan club in all of the English-speaking world, due in part to his magnificent voice that makes everything he writes come alive with a sense of excitement.

In the 1930s, Auden had been touted by academics as a strong candidate for the title of best of the Century but the free-wheeling spirit after the war made his poems no longer in fashion. There was never any denying his talent but his fall from favour was demonstrated in his fifth-place finish, far behind the major contenders.

The minimal support for the two female poets in the top ten was disappointing but it must be conceded the Century did not produce an Elizabeth Barrett Browning.

Champions of Your Century 1900 – 1999
BEST POET

1	T. S. Eliot	1,027 votes
2	John Betjeman	634 votes
3	Rudyard Kipling	456 votes
4	Dylan Thomas	312 votes
5	W. H. Auden	185 votes
6	W. B. Yeats	164 votes
7	Sylvia Plath	157 votes
8	Stevie Smith	144 votes
9	Philip Larkin	143 votes
10	Dannie Abse	106 votes

Chapter Twenty-one

Champions of Your Century : 1900 – 1999

GREATEST POP SINGERS, MALE and FEMALE

Elvis Presley has been voted the greatest male pop singer of the Century. His main challengers were Frank Sinatra, Elton John and Cliff Richard.

The superstar of the 1990s, Celine Dion, was chosen the greatest female pop singer of the Century.

Elvis has been called The King of rock for almost half a Century and for good reason. He has sold more albums than any other performer.

Elton John and Sinatra are next in total album sales and so the voters in Leicestershire and Rutland seem to be in tune with the rest of the English-speaking world in selecting the champions.

Cliff Richard was the first major rock soloist in Britain and will always be remembered for The Young Ones and for his spontaneous concert at Wimbledon during a rain delay.

Elton John has the satisfaction of singing the best-selling single of the Century, a tribute to Princess Diana.

Celine Dion turned back a challenge from Madonna with the help of her mega-hit from the Titanic, My Heart Will Go On. The song was a driving force behind the success of the film, which won eleven Oscars.

Celine might have been able to win without that song, but it would have been closer.

The controversial Madonna, who varied between brilliant and bizarre during her career, won respect with a surprisingly-good portrayal of Evita in the Andrew Lloyd Webber film musical but the emotion of Dion's Titanic song proved overwhelming in the final months of the Century.

In third place was Whitney Houston who had one of the top hits of the Century with her stunning rendition of I Will Always Love You.

For most of the Century in America the spotlight had been on Barbra Streisand and Judy Garland. People argued for years about who would win the title as the best of all time.

They first met when a very young Barbra was a guest on the Judy Garland television show when the colour was black and white and everything was live. There was no way to edit out what they said to each other at the end of their duet.

Celine Dion. (Photo courtesy David Pomona, Pomona Music.)

Elvis Presley, in *Roustabout* (1964, Paramount Pictures)

Champions of Your Century 1900 – 1999
BEST FEMALE POP SINGER

1	**Celine Dion**	*790 votes*
2	**Madonna**	*712 votes*
3	**Whitney Houston**	*543 votes*
4	**Barbra Streisand**	*535 votes*
5	**Julie Andrews**	*404 votes*
6	**Shirley Bassey**	*381 votes*
7	**Vera Lynn**	*334 votes*
8	**Judy Garland**	*321 votes*
9	**Tina Turner**	*320 votes*
10	**Karen Carpenter**	*122 votes*

Garland, recognising a threat when she saw one, walked up to Barbra and said: "You're so good I hate you."

Barbra smiled and replied: "I've hated you for years."

They both expected to be named first or second best female pop singer of the Century and they were never confident about who would be the champion.

As far as the voters in Leicestershire and Rutland are concerned, the answer was neither. But they both made an impact in our top ten.

The well-loved Shirley Bassey did well and the voters also remembered two great stars from the past, Julie Andrews and Vera Lynn.

After the top four male stars, three band members made a strong showing. John Lennon and Paul McCartney of The Beatles finished fifth and sixth as solo performers while Queen lead singer Freddie Mercury came seventh.

The Welsh favourite, Tom Jones, was eighth.

The surprise of the voting was the complete fall from grace of Michael Jackson, who dominated the music world in the 1980s but finished last in our election.

This category proved to be the most dynamic of all sixteen to date with heavy voting right to the final day. Only the race for top male comedian had a closer finish.

In any event, with your help we now have elected sixteen champions of the century. We salute them all.

Photos: Celine Dion photo courtesy David Pomona, Pomona Music;.Madonna in Dick Tracy, Touchstone Pictures. All rights reserved. Photograph by Peter Sorel; Barbra Streisand photo courtesy BBC; Whitney Houston photo courtesy BMG/Arista; Julie Andrews in The Sound of Music, 1965, 20th Century Fox. Tina Turner photo courtesy EMI Parlaphone.

Champions of Your Century 1900 – 1999
BEST MALE POP SINGER

1	Elvis Presley	857 votes
2	Frank Sinatra	729 votes
3	Elton John	661 votes
4	Cliff Richard	622 votes
5	John Lennon	496 votes
6	Paul McCartney	453 votes
7	Freddie Mercury	409 votes
8	Tom Jones	236 votes
9	Bryan Adams	216 votes
10	Michael Jackson	103 votes

Photos: Elvis Presley photo courtesy BMG Ent.; Cliff Richard, John Lennon and Paul McCartney photos from Leicester Mercury; Freddie Mercury photo courtesy Queen Productions; Michael Jackson photo courtesy EMI.

Index

Photograph entries are denoted with an asterisk

101 Dalmations: 38*, 89, 90*
1994, film: *66
1994, novel: 61, 62, 76

A
ABBA: 32, 33, 34*, 35, 55, 83*
Abbott and Costello: 16, 17, 19*
Abbott, Bud : 16, 17, 19*
Abdication of Edward VIII, The: 67*
Abse, Dannie: 58*, 59, 63, 93*
Absolutely Fabulous: 12, 86
AC/DC: 33, 34*
Adams, Bryan: 54, 55, 97, 97*
Adventures of Robin Hood, The: 44, 46
Aerosmith: 32*, 33, 35, 83*
African Queen, The: 44, 48, 67, 69*
Ahern, Caroline: 12, 13*
Airplane: 48
Aladdin: 39*
Albert the Lion: 29
Alice in Wonderland: 38
Alien: 42
Aliens 2: 48
All Day and All of the Night: 34
All This and Heaven Too: 48
Allen, Dave: 20, 21
Allen, Gracie: 18, 20
Alsatian: 24
Amadeus: 41, 48
Amapola: 31
American in Paris, An: 36, 45
Anastasia: 45*, 75*
Anchors Aweigh: 37, 43, 45
Andrews, Dana: 43
Andrews, Julie: 36, 45*, 53*, 54, 55, 88, 89*, 96*, 97
Annie Hall: 42
Apollo 13: 48
Aristocats, The: 39
Armstrong, Louis: 54
As Time Goes By: 7, 29, 30
Ashbery, John: 59
Askey, Arthur: 20
Astaire, Fred: 36, 43, 53, 69*
Atkinson, Rowan: 7*, 10*, 11, 21
Attenborough, Richard (Lord): 41, 45
Atwood, Margaret: 59
Auden, W.H.: 58, 59, 63*, 64, 93*
Austen, Jane: 42
Ave Maria: 15, 29
Ayres, Pam: 59, 62

B
Babe: 48
Babes on Broadway: 37
Ball, Lucille: 13, 14*, 20, 86, 87*
Bambi: 38*, 39, 48, 89, 90*
Bancroft, Anne: 68
Band, The: 33
Bare Necessities of Life, The: 89
Barker, Ronnie: 8*, 10, 16*, 21*
Barraclough, Roy 19, 21, 79, 80
Barrett, Syd: 34*
Barrymore, Michael: 11, 21
Basinger, Kim: 68*
Bassett Hound: 25*
Bassey, Shirley: 16, 54, 55, 56*, 96*, 97
Batman: 48
Battle of Britain: 48
Baxter, Stanley: 21
Beach Boys, The: 32*, 33, 34, 35, 83*
Beagle: 25
Beatles, The: 32, 33, 35*, 34, 35, 36, 82*, 83* 97
Beauty and the Beast: 38, 39, 89, 90*
Bee Gees, The: 32, 33, 35, 37*, 83*
Becket: 52*, 73*
Belgian Shepherd: 25
Belloc, Hilaire: 64
Ben Hur (1906): 47
Ben Hur (1939): 41, 42*, 46, 47, 48*, 67*, 82*, 92, 93
Bentine, Michael: 16*

Bergman, Ingrid: 5, 40, 45*, 65*, 68, 69, 70, 72, 74*, 75*, 92*
Betjeman, John, Sir: 58*, 59, 62, 63, 64, 93*
Big: 46
Big Country, The: 44, 47
Biggest Aspidastra in the World, The: 15, 30
Bill Haley and his Comets: 32
Binyon, Laurence: 64
Birds of a Feather: 12
Birth of a Nation: 44
Bishop, Elizabeth: 61
Black Adder: 7*, 17*
Bless 'Em All: 31
Blitz: 27*
Blondie: 32, 33, 55, 57*
Blood Donor Sketch, The: 10
Blood Sweat and Tears: 33
Blue Hawaii: 37
Bogart, Humphrey: 42, 44, 66*, 67, 69*, 72, 73*, 92*
Bohemian Rhapsody: 35
Bolger, Ray: 89*
Bon Jovi 32*, 33, 34, 83*
Bonnie and Clyde: 43
Bonnie Scotland: 17*
Booth, Connie: 19, 79
Border Collie: 22, 24, 25, 76, 77*
Bosworth, Wally: 21
Boxer: 25, 26
Boyd, Stephen: 43
Boys Zone: 33
Branagh, Kenneth: 47, 68
Brando, Marlon: 37, 47, 48, 67*, 68, 70
Bremner, Rory: 8*, 11
Bridge on the River Kwai, The: 42
Bridges of Madison County, The: 67*
Bridget Jones' Diary: 61
Brief Encounter: 42, 48
Brightman, Sarah: 55, 57*
Brooke, Rupert: 58, 63*
Brooks, Louise: 70
Browing, Elizabeth Barrett: 93
Bryan, Dora: 12, 13*
Brynner, Yul: 45*, 46*, 67*, 89*
Bullitt: 48
Burgess, Anthony: 62, 63
Burnett, Carol: 13*
Burns and Allen: 18, 20
Burns, George: 18, 20
Burton, Richard: 14, 49, 50*, 51, 65, 66*, 67, 69*, 70, 73*, 83, 84*
Butch Cassidy and the Sundance Kid: 46
Byrds: 33

C
Cagney, James: 44, 68, 70, 73*
Caine, Michael: 68*, 69, 70, 73*
Cairn Terrier: 25*
Calamity Jane: 45, 48
Camelot: 48
Camus, Albert: 61
Cannon and Ball: 18
Can't Buy Me Love: 32
Carlisle, Elsie: 30
Carousel: 37, 46
Carpenter, Karen: 55, 96*
Carr, Carole: 55
Carrott, Jasper: 20, 21
Carry On Films: 10, 12, 85
Casablanca: 5, 30, 40, 42, 43, 44, 46, 47, 48, 67, 72, 73, 91, 92*
Castle, Roy: 18*, 19
Catch 22: 61
Catcher in the Rye: 61
Cats: 64
Cause Celeb: 61
Chang, Jung: 61
Chaplin, Charlie: 7, 10*, 11, 20, 85, 86*
Chaplin, Geraldine: 92*
Chapman, Graham: 18*, 19
Charge of the Light Brigade: 44
Chariots of Fire: 41, 44
Charles, Hugh: 29

Chattanooga Choo Choo: 30
Chesterton, G.K.: 64
Chevalier, Maurice: 49
Chocolate Soldier: 29
Church Going: 63
Churchill, Winston, Sir: 49*, 50, 51, 82, 83*, 84*
Cinderella: 38, 39*, 48, 89, 90*
Citizen Kane: 40, 41*, 42, 44, 67*, 92*
Clash: 33, 34
Clash of the Titans: 48
Cleese, John: 8, 10, 17*, 18*, 19, 20, 21, 79, 80*
Cleopatra: 69
Clooney, Rosemary: 55
Close Encounters of the Third Kind: 46
Cocker Spaniel: 22*, 25, 26
Cohan, George M.: 28
Cole, Nat King: 54
Collins, Pauline: 12
Collins, Phil: 52*, 54
Collinson and Breen: 20
Colman, Ronald: 51, 68
Colonel Bogey March: 29
Coming Home: 67*
Coming In On a Wing and a Prayer: 28, 29, 81*
Como, Perry: 54
Conley, Brian: 11
Connery, Sean: 5, 67*, 68*, 72*, 73*
Connolly, Billy: 11
Conrad, Joseph: 62, 63
Cookson, Catherine: 60*, 62, 78*
Cooper, Gary: 47, 68
Cooper, Gladys: 70
Cooper, Tommy: 10, 11*, 21, 85, 86*
Cope, Wendy: 64
Corbett, Ronnie: 8, 16*, 21*
Corgi: 24, 25, 26
Cornwall, Bernard: 61
Costello, Lou: 16, 17*,18
Crain, Jeanne: 43
Crawford, Joan: 67*
Crazy Gang, The: 17*, 18
Crosby, Bing: 18, 31, 36, 37, 39*, 46*, 53*, 54
Cure, The: 34
Curtis, Ian: 34

D
Dachshund: 23*, 25, 26*, 77*
Dalmatian: 26*
Dance with a Dolly with a Hole in Her Stocking: 31
Dances with Wolves: 46
Daniels, Bebe: 20
Davies, Alan: 11
Davis, Bette: 28, 68, 69, 70
Davis, Jr., Sammy: 53*, 55
Dawson and Barraclough: 18*, 19, 21, 79, 80*
Dawson, Les: 9*, 18*, 19, 20, 21, 79, 80, 85, 86*
Day, Doris: 48, 54, 55, 56
Day-Lewis, Daniel: 47
De Casalis, Jeanne: 20
De Gaulle, Charles: 49
de Havilland, Olivia: 68
de la Mare, Walter: 64
Dead End: 44
Dead Parrot Sketch, The: 10
Dear Brigitte: 68*
Deayton, Angus: 11*
Deck of Cards: 29
Dee, Jack: 8*, 11
Deep Purple: 33, 34*
Deerhound: 26*
Deerhunter, The: 44, 48
Dench, Judy (Dame): 43
Desk Set: 50*
Diamonds are Forever: 73
DiCaprio, Leonardo: 43*, 70*
Dietrich, Marlene: 30, 55
Dion, Celine: 43, 53, 54*, 55, 56, 94*, 96*

Dire Straits: 33, 34
Disney films: 38-39*, 48*, 92*
Disney, Walt: 38, 48
Doberman: 25
Dodd, Ken: 11, 19*, 20, 21, 86*
Don't Look Now: 46
Doors, The: 32, 33, 34, 83*
Do-Re-Mi: 88
Double Indemnity: 46
Douglas, Kirk: 48
Dr. Zhivago: 42, 44, 46, 47, 48, 92*, 93
Dumbo: 38*, 89, 90*
Durban, Deanna: 43
Durham, Judith: 55
Dylan, Bob: 54

E
E.T.: 42, 44, 46
Eagles: 33
Earth Wind & Fire: 33
Easter Parade: 43, 44
Eastwood, Clint: 67*
Eddy, Nelson: 37
El Dorado: 67*
Electric Prunes: 34
Eliot, T.S.: 58*, 59, 62, 63, 64, 91, 93*
Elizabeth R: 51*
Elliott, Denholm: 47
Elmer Gantry: 42
Elvis- That's The Way It Is: 56*
Enemy Mine: 48
English Patient, The: 41, 45*
English Rose: 34
English Setter: 25
English Springer Spaniel: 23*, 24, 77*
Epithalamian: 59, 63
Eurythmics: 33, 34*
Evans, Norman: 21
Evita: 36, 45, 46, 94

F
Family Way, The: 10
Fancy Pants: 7
Fanny and Alexander: 46
Fantasia: 38, 39*, 44, 48
Faulkner, William: 62
Fawlty Towers: 10, 12, 17*, 18, 79, 80*, 86
Faye, Alice: 30, 55
Fiddler on the Roof: 37*
Field, Sid: 8
Fielding, Helen: 61
Fields, Gracie: 12*, 14, 15*, 20, 28, 29*, 30, 51, 54, 55, 80, 81*, 86, 87*
Fiennes, Joseph: 92*
Fiennes, Ralph: 45*
Firefighters: 27*
Fire Hall Sketch: 8
Fitzgerald, Ella: 54, 55, 56
Fitzgerald, F. Scott: 61, 62
Flanagan and Allen: 17*, 18, 29
Fleetwood Mac: 32, 33
Flying Down to Rio: 37
Flynn, Errol: 44
Fonda, Henry: 68
Fonda, Jane: 67*, 68, 69
Ford, Harrison: 55*, 68, 72, 73*
Foreigner: 33
Formby, George: 8, 20*, 21, 29, 31*, 30, 80, 81*
Forrest Gump: 41, 45*
Forsyth, Bruce: 11
Four Weddings and a Funeral: 5, 40*, 42, 43, 92, 92*, 93
Fox and the Hound, The: 39
Fox Terrier, smooth-haired: 24
French and Saunders: 12, 17*, 19, 21, 79,, 80*, 86
French Lieutenant's Woman: 65*
French, Dawn: 12*, 20, 21, 86, 87*
Frinton, Freddie: 20
Frost, Robert: 59
Funny Face: 69*
Funny Girl: 37

G

Gable, Clark: 5, 40*, 44, 68, 73*, 91*, 92*
Gallagher and Shean: 18
Gandhi, film: 41*
Gandhi, Mahatma: 49*, 84*
Garbo, Greta: 65*, 69
Garland, Judy: 30, 36, 37, 38, 45*, 48, 53*, 54, 55, 88, 94, 96*
Garson, Greer: 67*, 68
Gas masks: 28*
General, The: 44
Genesis: 52*
George, Lloyd: 49
German Shepherd: 23, 24, 25*, 76, 77*
Ghost: 42
Gielgud, John, Sir: 49
Gigi: 36, 42, 45, 89
Gilliam, Terry: 18*
Girl in the Alice Blue Gown: 30
Glen Miller Story, The: 37, 45, 48
Glenn Miller Band: 29, 30, 79, 81*
Glitter Band: 35
Godfather 2: 47
Godfather, The: 41, 44, 67*
Gold Rush: 7
Golden Retriever: 24, 25, 76*, 77*
Golding, William: 61
Gone with the Wind (film): 5, 12, 13, 40*, 41, 42, 43, 44, 46, 47, 48, 65*, 73, 91*, 92*
Gone with the Wind (novel): 61
Goodnight Sweetheart: 29
Goon Show, The: 16*, 19, 20, 79, 80*
Grable, Betty: 37, 67*
Graceland Museum: 57
Graduate, The: 46
Graham, Billy: 49
Grahame, Kenneth: 61
Grand Hotel: 65*
Grant, Cary: 51, 65, 67, 69, 70, 72, 73*
Grant, Hugh: 5, 40*, 43, 68, 92*
Grapes of Wrath, The (film and novel): 60, 61, 62
Graves, Robert: 62
Grayson, Kathryn: 37
Grease: 37, 44*, 46, 88, 89*
Great Dane: 22*, 24
Greatest Rory Ever Told, The: 8
Greatest Show on Earth, The: 43
Greatest Story Ever Told, The: 44
Greene, Graham: 60*, 62, 63, 78*
Grenfell, Joyce: 12, 13*, 20, 21, 87*
Griffith, Melanie: 5
Guinness, Alec, Sir: 68
Guns 'N' Roses: 34, 35
Guys and Dolls: 37, 48

H

Hale and Pace: 20:
Haley, Bill: 34:
Hancock, Tony: 9, 19*, 20, 21, 86*
Hancock's Half Hour: 19*
Handley, Tommy: 10
Hanks, Tom: 45*
Hard Day's Night, A, (film): 36, 44, 89
Hard Day's Night, A, (song): 34
Hardy, Oliver: 7, 20:
Hardy, Thomas: 59, 62, 63, 78
Harrison, Rex: 36*, 89*
Harry, Debby: 55, 57*
Hayes, Helen: 45*
Haymes, Dick: 59
Haynet, Arthur: 23
Hayward, Susan: 67*, 68, 69, 70
Hayworth, Rita: 43
Heald, Anthony: 68*
Heaney, Seamus: 59, 63
Hear My Song: 30
Hearne, Richard: 8
Heart: 33
Heller, Joseph: 61, 62
Hello, Frisco, Hello: 30
Help, film: 36
Help, song: 32, 33
Hemingway, Ernest: 60*, 62, 78*
Hendrix, Jimi: 35
Henry V: 47
Hepburn, Audrey: 36*, 68, 69*, 70, 72, 74, 74*, 89*
Hepburn, Katharine: 50*, 51, 68, 69*, 70, 72, 74*
Hercules: 39
Heston, Charlton: 42*, 43, 47, 67*, 68, 92*

Hey Jude: 32, 33
High Noon: 44, 47
High Sierra: 44
High Society: 37, 39*, 45
Highlander, The: 46
Hill, Benny: 9*, 20*, 21, 85*, 86*
Hill, Geoffrey: 59
Hoffman, Dustin: 68
Holden, William: 68
Holiday, Billie: 56
Holly, Buddy: 54
Home Guard: 28*
Hope and Crosby: 18, 80*
Hope, Bob: 7*, 18, 21, 51, 85, 86*
Hopkins, Anthony, Sir: 51, 68, 70*, 72, 73*
Horne, Lena: 54, 56
Houston, Whitney: 54*, 55, 56, 94, 96*
Howard, Leslie: 40*
Howard, Sidney: 12*
Howerd, Frankie: 7, 9*, 10, 20, 86*
Hughes, Ted: 59, 63
Humperdinck, Engelbert: 53*
Hunchback of Notre Dame, The: 39*
Husky: 24, 26*
Hunt for Red October, The: 68*
Huxley, Aldous: 61, 62

I

I Can't Get No Satisfaction 34
I Don't Know Why: 29
I Feel Fine: 33
I Had Too Much to Dream Last Night: 34
I Haven't Said Thanks for that Lovely Weekend: 29
I Love Lucy Show: 13
I Need You: 34
I Want to Hold Your Hand: 32, 33
I Will Always Love You: 94
I'll Be Seeing You: 28, 30, 81*
I'll Never Smile Again: 30
I'll Walk Alone: 28, 29, 30
I'm Not Like Everybody Else: 34
I'm Sending You the Siegfried Line to Hang Your Washing On: 30
Imre, Celia: 12
In My Life: 33
In the City: 34
In the Heat of the Night: 44
In the Mood: 27, 29, 79, 80, 81
Incredible Sarah : 70*
Inn of the Sixth Happiness: 44, 65*
Invasion of the Body Snatchers: 44
Irish Wolfhound: 25*
Irons, Jeremy: 68
It Happened One Night: 42, 48
Italian Greyhound: 25*
It's a Long Way to Tipperary: 28, 30
It's a Wonderful Life: 42, 44
It's That Man Again: 8
It's Twelve and a Tanner a Bottle, That's All That It's costing Tay Day: 30

J

Jack in the Beanstalk: 17*
Jack Russell: 25*
Jackley, Nat: 21
Jackson, Glenda: 18*, 49, 51*, 68, 74*, 84*
Jackson, Michael: 34, 52*, 54, 55, 57, 97*
Jacques, Hattie: 12
Jagger, Mick: 32, 53*, 54, 57
Jam, The: 34*
James and the Giant Peach 50
James Bond: 5, 68*, 72, 73*
James, Henry: 62, 63
James, Jimmy: 18
James, Sid: 9
Jaws: 42
Jazz Singer, The : 37*
Jefferson Airplane: 33
Jellico Cats: 59
Jennings, Elizabeth: 64
Jesus Christ Superstar: 36
John, Elton, Sir: 52*, 53, 55, 57, 94, 97*
Jolson Story, The: 37, 43
Jolson, Al: 37*, 53*, 54
Jones, Tom: 52*, 53, 55, 57, 97*
Joseph Lock: 30
Joseph, Jenny: 59
Joy Division: 34
Joyce, James: 61, 62, 63, 64*, 76, 78*
Jumanji: 48
Jungle Book, The: 39, 48*, 89*, 90*
Jurassic Park: 44, 48

Jurassic Park 2: 48

K

Kafka, Franz: 61
Kaye, Danny: 8, 37, 46*
Keel, Howard: 53, 57
Keep Right on to the End of the Road: 30
Keep the Home Fires Burning: 81
Keith, Penelope: 12, 21*
Kelly, Gene: 36*, 37, 89*
Kennedy, Jimmy: 30
Kennedy, John F. 51, 51*, 84*
Kennedy, Robert: 50
Kerouac, Jack: 61
Kerr, Deborah: 46*, 68, 70*, 74*, 89*
King and I, The: 37, 44, 45, 46*, 47, 48, 67*, 89*
King Charles Spaniel: 22*, 25
King George VI: 8
King, Jr., Martin Luther: 49, 51*, 82*, 84*
Kingsley, Ben: 41*, 68
Kinks, The: 33
Kipling, Rudyard: 58*, 59, 62, 64, 93*
Kiss: 33
Kiss Me Goodnight Sergeant Major: 30
Koestler, Arthur: 62
Korman, Harvey: 13
Kramer vs Kramer: 41

L

Labrador : 22*, 23*, 24, 25, 76*, 77*
Lady and the Tramp: 38*, 89, 90*
Laine, Cleo: 55, 57*
Lambeth Walk: 29
Lancaster, Burt: 68*
Lanza, Mario: 54, 57
Lara's Theme: 42
Larkin, Philip: 58, 59*, 63, 93*
Lassie Come Home: 42
Laurel and Hardy: 7, 17*, 18, 19, 20, 21, 80*
Laurel, Stan : 7*, 18
Lawrence of Arabia: 5, 41, 42, 44, 48, 92, 93
Lawrence, D.H.: 62, 63, 76, 78*
Lay Down Your Arms: 29
Leaning on a Lamp Post: 29, 30, 80, 81*
Lean, David Sir?: 5, 42, 47
Led Zeppelin: 33
Lee, Harper: 61
Lee, Peggy: 56
Leicester Arts Festival: 56*
Leicestershire Soldiers and Sailors: 30
Leigh, Vivien: 44, 46, 51, 65*, 68, 73, 74*, 91*, 92*
Lemmon, Jack: 20, 68
Lenin, V.I.: 49
Lennon, John: 53*, 54, 55, 57, 97*
Lennox, Annie: 55
Let It Be: 33
Lewis, C.S.: 61, 62, 78
Lewis, Jerry: 18
Life with the Lyons: 20
Lift, The: 8
Lili Marlene: 30, 31
Lion King, The: 38, 39, 88, 89*, 90*
Lipman, Maureen: 12*, 19, 87*
Little and Large: 18, 21
Brown, James (as *Darth Vader*): 92*
Little Brown Jug: 30
Little Mermaid, The: 39*
Little Stick of Blackpool Rock: 29
Little Tich: 8
Lloyd Webber, Andrew (Lord): 36, 93, 94
London Fantasy: 29
London, Julie: 55
Long Ago and Far Away: 28, 30
Long and Winding Road, The: 33
Lord of the Rings, The: 61
Lord, Jon: 34*
Love is a Many-Splendored Thing: 44
Love Me or Leave Me: 45, 48
Love Me Tender: 56*
Love, Bessie : 12
Lovely Day Tomorrow, A: 29
Lowell, Robert: 59
Lowry, Malcolm: 62
Lucan and McShane: 20
Lumley, Joanna: 12, 13*, 87*
Lurcher: 24
Lynn, Vera (Dame): 14, 28, 30, 54*, 55, 79, 81*, 96*, 97
Lyon, Benny: 20

M

MacLaine, Shirley: 68, 69
Madness of King George, The: 48
Madonna: 46, 54*, 55, 56, 94, 96*
Maginot Line, The: 30
Magnificent Ambersons, The: 46
Magnificent Seven, The: 44
Maltese Falcon, The: 44
Man for All Seasons, A: 47
Manic Street Preachers: 34
Many Adventures of Winnie the Pooh, The: 38, 39*
Manzarack, Ray: 34
Marquez, Gabriel Marcia: 61
Martin and Lewis: 18
Martin, Dean: 18
Martindale, Wink: 29
Marx Brothers (Groucho, Chico, Harpo): 16, 18*, 79, 80*
Marx, Groucho: 16
Mary Poppins: 36, 44, 45*, 47, 88, 89*
Mason, Nick: 34*
Matthau, Walter: 20
Maytime: 37, 45, 47
McCartney, Paul, Sir: 54, 55, 56*, 97*
McDonald, Jeanette: 37
McGough, Roger: 59, 64*
Meat Loaf: 33
Meet Me in St. Louis: 46, 48
Mercury, Freddie: 33, 35, 52*, 54, 55, 97*
Merman, Ethel: 54
Merton, Paul: 8*, 11
Metallica: 34
Mexican Hairless: 22*
Militiamen: 27*
Miller, Glenn: 27, 29, 30, 31*, 79, 81*
Miller, Max: 7, 8*, 10, 20, 21, 85, 86*
Milligan, Spike: 16*
Mills, Hayley: 70
Mills, John (Sir): 10
Milne, A.A.: 61
Minnelli, Liza: 55, 57*
Miranda, Carmen: 37
Mitchell, Margaret: 40, 61, 91, 92
Mitchum, Robert: 68, 69
Mongrel, faithful: 23*, 25, 26
Monkhouse, Bob: 9, 20*
Monroe, Marilyn: 65*, 68, 69, 70, 74*
Monty Python: 10, 18*, 19, 21, 79, 80*
Moonlight Cocktail: 29
Moonlight Serenade: 29
Moore, Marianne: 59
Morecambe and Wise: 16, 18*, 19, 20, 21, 79*, 80*
Morecambe, Eric: 7, 11, 18*, 21
Moreno, Rita: 36*, 89*
Morrison, Jim: 34
Mr. Bean: 11
Mr. Hulot's Holiday: 44
Mr. Pastry: 8
Mrs. Merton: 12, 13*
Mrs. Miniver: 42, 43
Murray, Les: 59, 63
My Fair Lady: 36*, 42, 44, 47, 88, 89*
My Heart Will Go On: 43, 54, 94

N

Nabokov, Vladimir: 62
Name of the Rose, The: 72*
Nat Mills and Bobby: 20
National Velvet: 42
Naughty Marietta: 37, 45, 47
New Moon: 37
News of the World: 34
Newton John, Olivia: 36, 55, 88, 89*
Nichols, Mike: 50
Nicholson, Jack: 68
Nielson, Leslie: 48
Nightingale Sang in Berkeley Square, A: 29, 30
Nirvana: 34
No, Honestly: 12
Northwest Passage: 46
Not Waving But Drowning: 59, 63
Novarro, Ramon: 47

O

Oasis: 32*, 33, 34, 83*
O'Connor, Des: 11
Odd Couple, The: 20
Oh, Johnny, Oh, Johnny. Oh!: 30
Oklahoma: 37, 45
Old Dark Horse, The: 44
Old English Sheepdog: 23*, 77*
Old Mother Riley and Kitty: 20

Oliver!: 36, 42, 44, 47
Olivier, Laurence (Lord): 49, 50*, 51, 68, 70*, 84*
Omen 3: 48
On the Road to Mandalay: 59
On the Waterfront: 42, 47
One Hundred Years of Solitude: 61
Open All Hours: 10
Orators, The: 59
Orwell, George: 50, 60*, 61, 62, 63, 76, 78*
O'Shea, Tessie (*Two Ton Tessie*): 12
O'Toole, Peter: 5, 66*, 92
Out of Africa: 44
Over the Garden Wall: 21
Over the Rainbow: 38
Over There: 28, 30
Owen, Wilfred: 64

P

Pack Up Your Troubles in Your Old Kit Bag and Smile, Smile, Smile: 28, 30
Page, Geraldine: 68
Page, Lynda: 61*
Paige, Elaine: 55
Paint Your Wagon: 47
Palin, Michael: 18*
Paltrow, Gwyneth: 92*
Parker, Ross: 29
Parsons, Nicholas 22*, 21
Partridge, Alan: 11
Pasquale, Joe: 11*
Payne, John: 37
Peck, Gregory: 68
Pennsylvania 6-5000: 30
Pet Shop Boys: 55
Peter Pan: 38, 39*
Phantom of the Opera: 57*
Piaf, Edith: 55, 56
Picnic at Hanging Rock: 46
Pink Floyd: 33, 34*
Pinocchio: 38, 39*, 89, 90*
Plath, Sylvia: 59, 62, 63, 93*
Pocahontas: 39*
Poem in October: 63
Poems (Auden): 59
Poitier, Sidney: 44, 68
Police: 32*
Poodle, Standard: 25
Porridge: 8*, 10
Porter, Cole: 37
Pound, Ezra: 59
Praise the Lord and Pass the Ammunition: 28
Predator: 48
Presley, Elvis: 36, 37, 52, 53, 55, 56*, 57, 94, 95*, 97*
Previn, Andre: 16
Prime of Miss Jean Brodie: 48
Princess Diana: 51
Procul Harum: 35
Psycho: 44, 46
Pug: 24
Punk Rock: 34

Q

Queen: 34. 35, 35*, 83*, 97
Queen Elizabeth II: 49*, 51, 83, 84*
Queen Mother: 18
Quiet Man, The: 43, 48
Quirk, Pauline: 12

R

R. E. M.: 33, 34
Radiohead: 34
Raiders of the Lost Ark: 42
Random Harvest: 43, 44
Read, Beryl: 20
Rear Window: 43
Rebecca: 48
Red Sails in the Sunset: 15
Redford, Robert: 68
Redgrave, Vanessa: 68
Rescuers, The: 39
Revnell, Ethel: 20
Rhodes, Marjorie: 10
Richard III: 50*
Richard, Cliff, Sir: 36, 52, 53, 55, 56*, 57, 94, 97*
Richardson, Ralph, Sir: 49

Roach, Hal: 21
Road Films: 18
Roberts, Julia: 69, 70
Robin Hood: 39
Robson, Linda: 12
Rock Around the Clock: 32
Rocky: 41
Rodgers and Hammerstein: 37
Roger Rabbit: 42
Rogers, Ginger: 36
Roll Out the Barrel: 30, 31, 81*
Rolling Stones, The: 32, 35, 83
Room with a View, A: 47
Rooney, Mickey: 37
Roosevelt, Franklin Delano (FDR): 49*, 51, 84*
Roper, George: 20
Rose Marie: 47
Ross, Diana: 55, 56
Rough Collie: 24, 25*
Roustabout: 95*
Rubettes: 35
Run Rabbit Run: 29, 30
Rush: 33
Rutherford, Margaret: 20
Ryan's Daughter: 44

S

Sachs, Andrew: 10, 19, 79
Salinger, J.D.: 61, 64*
Sally: 15, 30
Saratoga: 66*
Sassoon, Sigfried: 64
Saunders, Jennifer: 12, 20, 21*, 86, 87*
Saving Private Ryan: 46
Scales, Prunella: 12, 19, 20, 21, 23*, 79, 86, 87*
Scott Thomas, Kristin: 40*, 45, 92*
Scott, Terry: 21
Scream: 48
Sea Hawk, The: 44
Searchers, The: 46
Secombe, Harry, Sir: 16*
See What the Boys in the Backroom Will Have: 30
Sellers, Peter: 7*, 9, 10, 16, 20, 85, 86*
Selznick, David O.: 91, 92
Sense and Sensibility: 42
Serenade in Blue: 29, 30
Seven Brides for Seven Brothers: 43, 45
Sex Pistols: 33
Sgt.Pepper's Lonely Hearts Club Band: 32
Shadows, The: 48
Shakespeare in Love: 43, 91, 92*
Shakespeare, William: 43
Sharif, Omar: 5
Sharpe novels: 61
Shawshank Redemption, The: 44
She Loves You: 32, 33
Shelton, Anne: 55
Shipyard Sally: 12*
Shirley Valentine: 42, 48
Shitsu: 26
Shooting Party, The: 47
Shore, Dinah: 28, 54, 55
Showaddywaddy: 35*, 83*
Silence of the Lambs, The: 68*
Silver Wings in the Moonlight: 31:
Silvers, Phil: 22:
Simple Minds: 35:
Simply Red: 34:
Sims, Joan: 14:
Sinatra, Frank: 28, 36, 37*, 48, 53, 55*, 56, 57, 94, 97*:
Sing as We Go: 32:
Singin' in the Rain: 36*, 43, 44, 46, 47, 48, 88, 89*
Sleeping Beauty: 40:
Sleuth: 68*:
Smashing Pumpkins: 36:
Smith, Maggie: 47, 70:
Smith, Stevie: 59, 63, 93
Smoke Gets in Your Eyes: 18:
Snow White and the Seven Dwarfs: 38, 39, 48*, 89, 90*
Some Like It Hot: 42
Something's Got to Give (unfinished film): 65*

Songs for Swinging Lovers: 55
Sons and Lovers: 62
Sound of Music, The: 36, 37, 42, 43, 44, 46, 47*, 53*, 88*, 89*
South Pacific: 37, 45
Space Jam: 42
Spartacus: 48
Spender, Stephen, Sir: 58
Spice Girls, The: 52, 53, 55
Spring Parade: 43
Springfield, Dusty: 55
Springtime in the Rockies: 37
St. Bernard: 24, 25*, 77*
Stagecoach: 43
Stagedoor Canteen: 29
Stanwyck, Barbara: 70
Star Wars: 40*, 42, 43, 46, 47, 65*, 92*
Stardust: 48
State Fair: 43
Stateroom Scene: 16
Steely Dan: 33
Steiger, Rod: 44
Steinbeck, John: 60, 61, 62, 78*
Stevens, Wallace: 59
Stewart, James: 68*, 69, 73*
Sting: 34*
Sting, The: 44
Stone Roses: 34
Streep, Meryl: 40, 45*, 65*, 68, 69, 70, 72, 74*
Streisand, Barbra: 37, 54, 55, 56, 57*, 70, 94, 96*
String of Pearls: 30
Summer Holiday: 36, 48
Sun Also Rises, The (novel): 62
Supertramp: 33
Sword in the Stone, The: 38, 39*
Syal, Meera: 61

T

Take That: 33
Tarri, Suzette: 20
Tarzan of the Apes: 46
Taylor, Elizabeth: 13, 14, 65, 68, 69*, 70, 74*
Teddy Bear's Picnic: 29
Temple, Shirley: 38
These Days: 34
They're Either Too Young or Too Old: 28
Thing-ummy-Bob That's Going to Win the War, The: 14
Third Man, The: 46
This is the Army: 43
This is the Modern World: 34
This Is the Moment: 37
Thomas, Dylan: 49, 58, 59, 62, 63*, 64, 84*, 93*
Thomas, Edward: 59
Tibetan Spaniel: 25
Time Machine, The (1940) 49
Titanic: 41, 43*, 46, 54, 72, 91, 92*, 94
To Catch a Thief: 66*
To Kill a Mocking Bird (novel): 61
To the Manor Born: 12
Tolkien, J.R.R.: 61
Tom Jones, film: 42
Townsend, Sue: 61*
Tracy, Arthur (*The Street Singer*): 30
Tracy, Spencer: 68, 70
Trainspotting (novel): 61
Travolta, John: 36, 88, 89*
Trinder, Tommy: 8, 9, 20
Trolley Song, The: 30
Trollope, Joanna: 61
Troops at recreation: 28*
Tubeway Army: 34
Turner, Tina: 54*, 55, 96*
Tushingham, Rita: 70
Twelve Angry Men: 44
Two Ronnies: 10, 16*, 19, 21*, 79, 80*

U

U2: 32, 33, 34
UB40: 33
Ulysses: 61, 62
Underneath the Arches: 29, 30
Upper Lambourne: 63

V

Vance, Vivian: 14*
Vaughan, Sarah: 56
Velvet Underground: 33
Verve, The: 34
Vicar of Dibley: 12*, 21

W

Wabash Avenue: 67*
Wake of the Red Witch: 50*
Walker, Alice: 61
Wall, Max: 8*, 20
Walters, Julie: 13
War and Peace: 44, 46
Warsaw Concerto: 29
Waste Land, The: 59, 93
Water Spaniel: 23
Waters, Roger: 34*
Way You Look Tonight, The: 29
Wayne, John: 50*, 51, 67*, 68, 70
Weissmuller, Johnny: 46
We'll Meet Again: 14, 28, 29, 30, 79, 81*
Welles, Orson: 40, 41*, 42, 51, 67*, 92*
Wells, H.G.: 62, 63
Welsh, Irvine: 61
We're Going to Get Lit Up When the Lights Go On in London: 30
We're Going to Hang Out the Washing on the Siegfried Line: 30
Wesley, Mary: 61
West Highland Terrier: 24, 25*, 76, 77*
West Side Story: 36*, 37, 42, 45, 46, 89*
West, Gracie: 20
Wet Wet Wet: 33, 34*
Wham!: 33
What a Swell Party This Is: 37
What's the Good of a Birthday: 15
When Father Papered the Parlour: 29
When the Lights Go On Again: 30
When the Poppies Bloom Again: 29
Whippet: 24
White Christmas, film: 37, 45, 46*
White Christmas, song: 31
White Cliffs of Dover, The: 28, 29, 30, 79, 81
Who, The: 32
Who's Afraid of Virginia Woolf?: 42, 50
Who's on First?: 16
Who's Taking You Home Tonight: 29
Wild Swans: 61
Williams, William Carlos: 59
Wilton, Robb: 8
Windsor, Barbara: 12, 20, 21, 86, 87*
Winnie the Pooh: 38, 39*
Winslet, Kate: 43*, 69, 70*, 72, 74*
Wisdom, Norman 22
Wise, Ernie: 18*, 21
Wish Me Luck as You Wave Me Goodbye: 14, 28, 31, 80, 81*
Witness: 46
Wizard of Oz, The: 37, 38, 42, 44, 45*, 46, 47, 48, 88, 89*
Women's Land Army: 27*
Wood, Victoria: 7, 12*, 13, 19, 20, 21, 85, 87*
Woods, Eli: 18
Woolf, Virginia: 62, 63, 64*, 78*
Working Girl: 5, 42
Worth, Harry: 21
Wright, Rick: 34*

Y

Yankee Doodle Dandy: 37, 44
Yeats, W. B.: 59, 63*, 64, 93*
Yes: 33
Yesterday: 33
Yorkshire Terrier: 24, 25, 26, 77*
You Really Got Me: 34
You Were Never Lovelier 45
You'll Never Know: 30
You'll Never Walk Alone: 37
Young Ones, The: 36, 94
Yours: 29, 81*

Z

Zulu: 45